teresa fritschi

all that i need,

or live like a dog
with its head stuck out
the car window

Published 2011 by Teresa Fritschi

Library of Congress Cataloguing-in-Publication-Data
(application being processed)

Fritschi, Teresa A, 1961–

All That I Need, or live like a dog with its head stuck out the car window /by
Teresa A. Fritschi
Philosophy 2. Self-help 3. Memoir 4. Travel-log
5. Meditations on relevance -aging

ISBN 978-1466497788

For Doris and my swim coaches.

All things are possible with encouragement.

author's note

As with every book you've ever held in your hand, or read on an eReader,© there is a need for the author to acknowledge the individuals without whose influence the end product might not have been taken up, slaved over, revised or reviewed multiple times, there is no exception to be found here.

For good or ill, every person we encounter will change our lives as we allow it.

This book is dedicated to all the amazing people whose presence in my life, often even without their realization, has had, or continues to have, astonishing influence upon me. To every person who has cared to listen to my first person narrative and laughed, cried or expressed that my wisdom was far beyond my years (for many years)—a very inadequate thank you.

Though it might surprise him, my father defending the authenticity of my writing to both my 11th grade AP English teacher, Mr Paul Houser, who accused me of plagiarism on my term paper about *Ordinary People*© and gave me a failing grade, and then again to my high school principal Mr James Walline, defined my life in ways I have only just come to understand. I can still hear him say, 'she's driven me crazy reading each sentence she's re-written out loud throughout the entire Stanley Cup Playoffs; of course it's her work!' Different friends are now subjected to my revisions but that singular validation of 'me' with my unique gifts, my passion for choosing the right words to convey the most salient points of a story, my Pollyanna mind-set, has carried me through the last 34 years of my life.

For my very special friends, whose dreams so different from my own, cajoled and encouraged and could see The New York Times© Best Seller status and Oprah's Book Club,© and appearances on Rachel Ray© or Ellen© if only I would only write. Thank you, it matters not if you are right!

To the people, living and long since passed, to be found within these pages as well as those who I have failed to include, who in touching my life have made it richer, imparted wisdom or ignited curiosity at a moment that helped me grow as a person and now, subsequently, help me to underscore a point I hoped to have made providing deeper meaning to you the reader, oh, if you could only know how much I love all of you and wish you every happiness.

With a heart full of gratitude and in joy,

contents

foreword

Nostalgia . . . in the midst of the noise, the media, all of the technology it is easy to think life is different today than in the past. However, human beings are now and have always been the same. We have a deep desire to make a difference, be connected, love, especially be loved. The human condition has always been one of deep emotion and deep longing. Reading Teresa's book is like reading an invitation to a grand life party. You have the right to RSVP "no thanks" or "include me and I'll bring the wine." Living life as a grand invitation is so powerful because the mere word "YES!" actually puts a whole host of things in motion and especially synchronicity.

Teresa is one of my best friends and I can assure you that this book is largely autobiographical. I say that as one might read this as an art of fiction: a wide adventure based on someone's wild imagination. I assure you all of the coincidences, all of the miracles, all of the "no way!" stories are based in real life; Teresa models for us a way to truly embrace our inner child and live in "awe" and "wonder."

We are born curious, proud and believing we are special. At around fourth grade, we begin to internalize messages that we should not be that happy or that we are really not that special. I know this to be true as I have two daughters and have seen their light begin to flicker and wan as they get older. **All That I Need** can be a means for you to rekindle that inner knowing, that inner fire. My recommendation is that you get journal and capture your own experiences that are catalyzed as you read. I am a big believer in "write it down;

make it happen" and the very act of your reading and writing will allow your unconscious to surface as you get permission to dream and hope, once again.

What I also know for sure is that Teresa truly believes you deserve more happiness than you think you are entitled to. Each page was blessed with an intention that your experience of yourself become more apparent, appreciated and amplified. This is a book about you. One of my favorite poets Mary Oliver asks, "What is it you plan to do with your one wild and precious life?" Once you read **All That I Need** you will be much better prepared to answer.

Jennifer Sertl
Author, *Strategy, Leadership & the Soul*

introduction

Newport, Rhode Island, the perfect catch-up day location. Before she returns to Istanbul to take care of her aging mother my girlfriend Hilal takes the train down from Boston. I drive up from Connecticut to pick her up. We start the day with Eggs Benedict (or did we go straight to the three layer double chocolate cake?) at Annie's Diner. We hit every charming boutique—small purchases become mementoes of the day. Two Adirondack chairs on the green expanse of manicured lawn falling down to the impossibly blue sea reflecting tiny mirrors of afternoon sunlight wait for us at The Chanler at Cliff Walk. Cotton-batting clouds drift across a cornflower blue sky. Sleek, ridiculously expensive sailboats with billowing sails glide past us and the towering bridge. Planters Punch in oversized tumblers is brought down to us on a silver tray. At which point Hilal turns to me and says, "For someone with no money you sure know how to live." Can there be a finer compliment in the whole world?

I was driving my girlfriend Pam to the doctor's one day and we're chatting about nothing that I can specifically recall, but she says, "Sometimes I wish that I could just suck the way you think out of you and put it inside me." Again, can there be a finer compliment? I replied, "You'd be miserable without anything to worry about." We never really want what someone else has—the trick is to embrace and cultivate being the best we can be in our own skin. As she wasn't quite up to it on the way to the doctor's, I later shared with her that in that moment I had a visual flashback to the original *Star Trek*© series (we're both old enough to watch the episodes the first time around) and the salt alien. The salt alien changed shape to appear to Captain James T. Kirk ™ and his crew as what each most personally longed for—luring them into complaisance before attaching octopus like suction cupped 'fingers' to suck the salt out of their bodies. Resulting shared laughter was worth waiting for.

An ordinary man is seeking answers to how to live his life more fully. He enters the New Age bookstore and cafe in his neighbourhood. He picks up a Chai tea latte with rice milk (No. Really. He does!) and goes to the Self-Help section to browse. As he scans the stacks a beautiful cover with a white Lotus blossom on a watery blue-green ground with its title in swirly type-font in both English and Sanskrit jumps out at him. The title reads, 'Buddhism, a path to achieving bliss.' Tea in one hand he can't really scan the contents so he simply buys the book. When he gets outside he finds a park bench under a full canopied shade tree to sit and read. He pulls his book out and opens it, only to discover it is blank inside.

Of course, it's blank inside. Our lives aren't (perhaps shouldn't be) determined by the contents of any book. What we will be, how we live, those who we love, the impact we leave on the world after our physical being has passed, is entirely up to us. Steve Jobs, founder of Apple© died on the 5th of October 2011 at 56. We are not all going to shift the paradigm of hundreds of millions of people as Mr Jobs managed to. What's more important is living as an example of passion and commitment. Jobs and Randy Pausch (1960–2008) of *The Last Lecture*© both chose to fully embrace positively impacting others' lives even as they were dying of pancreatic cancer.

desperation
1. Loss of hope and surrender to despair
2. A state of hopelessness leading to rashness

Hmm. Rashness. Hasty, ill-conceived action. It's clear from the way they lived their lives, with purpose and clarity of thought, that desperation was unlikely to be known to either Messieurs Jobs or Pausch. I think about people grasping for attention, racing from the latest diet craze to extreme exercise/fitness, hypochondria, meditation and yoga, the cult of religious or shopping fanaticism seeking salvation from the tiny hollow spots within us and wonder how can there possibly be so much pain in the world? How is it possible to get so lost in pursuit of mitigating the void that you cease to appreciate beauty; especially, that which is reflected in the mirror as you brush your teeth every morning? You think that 'no one knows' the angst you suffer; shuffling the cards then holding them tightly, you think the Poker face you wear conceals the state of your affairs, mind and heart be assured it doesn't; your pain is obvious to everyone around you. If your friends and family are enabling you—shame on them. But the real truth is that they can't help you, only you have that power. Like any illness, admitting that you have a problem is the first step toward recovery or finding peace. Like the fictitious book above, the whole point of **All That I Need** is just that.

Who we are, what we need, is already inside of us. The wisdom is there, waiting. All of our lives are assigned a finite number of days to enjoy—and we never know when our last will be. Even if you are not seeking answers to the great questions of our age, you need to recognise that what we need to thrive exists within us—we need only to listen with our heart for the answers. I believe we were all born with this wisdom, yet we have somehow disconnected from our essence. We all simply need to slow down, stop racing around, looking to experts to help us find happiness, cease looking at the world as unfair, too hard. Breathe!

Why am I writing this book? I can say honestly that since commencing work on **All That I Need**, every time I have read this question the answer has been different. What remains is that this is a book I have been encouraged to write for many years, my response consistently having been 'who would want to read what I have to say?' But the truth is that each and every one of us has a certain destiny to fulfill and our lives are only so long. My girlfriend Patricia often said that I have more serendipity in my life than anyone she's ever known. It's only partly true, I am just likely more aware of making odd connections. Like everyone else I have been known to put off fully embracing my talents, have denied my capabilities, or the value my efforts. Then somewhat mysteriously, subtle and then ever louder messages come at me in consistent intervals that despite my own (and the rest of humankind's) ability to exist in the status quo, suddenly it's no longer possible to do so. Nothing, at that point, makes anymore *sense* than the leap of faith often found in a Hollywood screen play. My psyche is suddenly keenly aware of my next métier, my life seemingly changes in the space of a breath despite the progressive path leading to a point of realization and action.

And so, on the 23rd of July 2011, in the span of time between 8:21 and 8:42 PM when I wrote what has become part of a chapter entitled *The Yoga Sprinter* on my BlackBerry™

and hit the send button, I was suddenly ready, though I still didn't *know it*. The communication was sent to a woman with whom I was barely acquainted, met over a couple of days at my health club, and her reaction took my breath away. Sharing my initial words and her reply with two of my dearest girlfriends, referenced further on as 'Diana's,' I was struck dumb by the immediacy of their responses and the content. I was forced to examine the heretofore unconscious value my words were bringing to people's lives. Those precise time stamps conveyed to me that quite clearly I needed to get out of my own way, sit down and start writing. Exactly three months, from start to completed (fully edited and formatted) manuscript. It hardly seems possible—especially if you as a reader understand that I do not have a caffeine jones!

On some level **All That I Need** is my own visceral reaction to the myriad of books about personal discovery, self-help, therapy, meditation, overcoming eating disorders, *The Secret*© and *The Power of Intention*© and *Eat, Pray, Love*© amongst them, all with the promised panacea to some kind of perfect life if only you follow the path outlined within. Really? Guess what, life isn't perfect. *Under The Tuscan Sun*© is a better example of 'making lemonade' and living your life fully and completely. Unfaithfulness, followed by the hedonistic enjoyment of fresh grapes, a gated, post-card pretty, falling down villa, bunches of lavender fighting scorpions, language barriers overcome with food and convivial laughter, and a dogged determination to make something beautiful out of what appeared to be a life in ruins. Why wouldn't we want to live our lives like that? If you were only caught up in the beauty of Frances Mayes' language and the faery tale ending of the movie screen play, read it again. Pay close attention to the frustration and details of all the work involved.

Life is as hard as you decide to make it, but passion will make the rough spots a whole lot easier to bear.

Certainly the momentary examples of my own 'life well lived' are spread out over a course of many years, so it would be unfair to let you assume the ideas herein took me a mere 22 minutes to formulate. I am certainly not, to use the current *nom de jour*, a Thought Leader, nor do I hold multiple advanced degrees in Theology or the Humanities; I am simply a participant in life with an acute sense of observation, especially when it comes to the human condition. I have been influenced, learned, left myself open to discovery from all of my experiences, some of which date from when I was six years old.

In each drafted chapter, shared with some twenty individuals represented within, I have discovered that my words found resonance and impacted the readers in unforeseen ways; circumstances often shifting to expand horizons professionally, personally and, yes, even romantically. Their nearly consistent refrains drove me onward to hopefully instill some measure of 'magic' beyond my immediate circle of influence.

A caveat: **All That I Need** is not a how-to guide. It won't make you rich, thin, or gorgeous (except, I hope, on the inside). It's unlikely you will have some great epiphany as a result of reading it. I doubt, though secretly I would love to be wrong on this point, that it will still be as relevant as William Makepeace Thackeray or Henry Fielding's work 300 years on. Maybe you will laugh or cry, reconnect with your inner child (if you lost that connection in the first place) but more than that, perhaps you will see possibilities and examples of how to stretch yourself to live in a little more fully each of the moments you have been granted.

Over lunch with our friend Amy, my girlfriend Jenn once announced to me that while they were 'Diana's' (that is to say the incarnate of the fabled Huntress), I was Aphrodite, the physical manifestation of love. Not the sexual love that 90% of you reading this will assume she meant—no, rather the clear, soft white Divine light associated with goodness and beauty. It is beauty, a complete reverence for transcendence, which drives my being, in touching it, observing it, capturing 'it' if only in my head, drawing others attention to its ephemeral nature, sometimes my being acknowledges that it has touched me with an outpouring of tears which makes my life complete.

With that in mind, maybe I can impart something here which will resonate within your own being, make perfect sense, allow you to be calmer, or vibrate with what you thought was a lost dynamism. I hope to help you retune yourselves to actually feel, and marvel, at your own breath, be a more positive influence to those around you, our planet, and especially yourself.

"A Country of Women," by Holly Morris, as featured in the April 2011 issue of *MORE Magazine*,© is a perfect illustration of resiliency. The tiny group known as the Babushkas of Chernobyl (some of you will only know the name as a result of the Fukushima Daiichi Nuclear Power Station partial meltdowns) have quite possibly endured more hardship than the combined population of a small country. Yet the tone of their interviews, their very ability to survive—let alone thrive—is inspiring. Bad things happen with less frequency than good things, but it seems all of humankind would prefer to focus on the pain, anger, sadness, abuse and then rally against the unfairness of it all.

You, dear reader, need to get over yourself. 'Poor Me Syndrome' carries no weight here.

And so, I am going to share some anecdotal stories about living in happiness.

I want **All That I Need** to shake your tree just a little, crack open your heart and your head to live more fully in every moment—something easily within all of our grasps just like low hanging fruit. If my words help you recognise not only the beauty within yourself but in the world around you, to be more conscious and take more sensual pleasure from the day-to-day living of your lives then I have accomplished more than was imagined as the first words were tapped out on my BlackBerry.

✧　✧　✧

Note to readers: The choice of spelling some words using British English is deliberate on my part—don't you think the word faery just looks more charming? Equally so I have (admittedly) taken certain liberties with grammar and punctuation conventions to place emphasis on a thought or convey the breathless monologue of teenagers (the urgency of which I regard as charming). Of course there is always the possibility of missing something and for those errors I take full responsibility.

teresa fritschi

all that i need,

or live like a dog
with its head stuck out
the car window

1 live like a dog with its head stuck out the car window

Michel de Montaigne (Essays, 1580) understood that his own nature was fully dependent upon his acquiescence to his dog's desire to play; "I am not afraid to admit that my nature is so tender, so childish, that I cannot well refuse my dog the play he offers me or asks of me outside the proper time."

A dog, most anyway, seem to live for pleasure. The constant shrill of a squeaky toy, however grating on human ears, can amuse a dog for *h-o-u-r-s*! The ordinary kitchen cupboard becomes a gravy train Nirvana stocked with rawhides and pig ears, peanut butter and doggie cookies which your dog will train you to fork over by letting you believe he's doing tricks to please you. His/her head goes into our lap, they look woefully at us to go for a walk for the sole purpose of chasing a squirrel or covering the scent of other dogs with his own. (Doesn't it astonish how much control they have over their bladders meting out a few drops here and there for nearly an hour long walk? Just how do they do that?)

There is but one supreme experience in a dog's life that exceeds all others, a ride in the car. My theory validated when putting the roof up on my convertible in a bank parking lot two dogs sat in the car parked next to mine; both became animated and curious over the roof. I couldn't help but smile at their reactions. When their owner came out I told him what had happened. Evidently their response was based upon personal doggie experience—the other family car is a convertible. Our dog friends live for moments like these. A dog begs to get into the car with you, either jumping into the passenger seat to ride shotgun (if a big dog) or if little (30 pounds or under) somehow winds up in your lap and waits for you, his 'stupid' human owner, to put the window down so he can stick his head out of it. (Technically speaking this isn't very safe for your best friend to do and really dumb for you as the driver of a car to allow. There are plenty of things our best (human) friends do which are equally dangerous but we/they are capable of making a cognitive choice based upon risk, capability and pleasure before they (insert activity of choice) our dog friends are not.) The level of dog pleasure is palpable as the wind currents dance around his/her head, the speed of the car blowing their ears straight back, their coat billowing to their shoulders, pink tongue cast to one side, and most of them smiling in a way human beings generally cease to do about age 9. Tell me honestly that you haven't also smiled at and wondered for years what each and every one of those dogs is thinking?

In many of our lives there was a time, however fleeting, when the greatest joy we could possess came from something quintessentially timeless and not very expensive; equal in every pleasurable way to a dog riding with his head out the car window. 'This stuff' tantalized our senses and filled us to overflowing with happiness. Like our dog friends we stuck our hands out car windows to make 'airplanes,' flying out over the water on a rope swing, having an older kid (thanks David Prawel) capture fireflies in a quart jar for us on a summer night, building snowmen, fireworks lighting up the sky, the banging away scaring us senseless and the culminating, cataclysmic smell of sulphur assaulting our noses, a grassy slope with leopard frogs leaping away in front of us as we rolled down the hill laughing, a new package of Crayola™ Crayons (wasn't it better if it was a box of 64 with the built in sharpener?) and a new colouring book, learning to swim (in my case in both the St. Lawrence River, near St. Regis Falls and Messina NY, and the Niagara River at the end of Sunset Drive), or the stereo playing Dad's vinyl collection of Credence Clearwater Revival (as weekend revelry at 7 AM) and Benny Goodman at more mellow times.

Our sense of taste satiated with vine-ripened deep red, juice-filled watermelon, hot chocolate covered with melting marshmallows on top, an orange Slurpee,® peppermint candy ice cream, steamed clams (my dad used to buy a bushel sized mesh bag at least once each summer) with fresh summer corn drowning in real butter with lemon wedges, popping as many red raspberries in our mouths as our greedy little hands could pluck from Grandpa's lush bushes, oh yes, and Crunchy Peter Pan® peanut butter on white bread thick with homemade strawberry jam and a really cold glass of milk! (Yes, I admit that I am one of those 'freaks' that absolutely love the taste of milk and especially how I feel after I drink it—diets be damned.)

The most remarkable gift of my life is that at the half century mark I retain the ability to experience the world with essentially same eyes as I did when I was six. I know. I am blessed. The same wonder, the same feeling of discovery like I am in on some mysterious secret, the indescribable pleasure of absolutely everything! The humility which can be manifest in discovering within myself that I am perfectly capable of doing something totally unexpected gives me not only the jolt of 'that was cool' but also 'what's next?'

What about you? When was the last time you took your casual observer status and derived pleasure from watching a child eating something amazing for the first time? Or something they love like Cheese Puffs® or chicken fingers. Have you ever talked to the birds and notice how they will 'talk' back to you if you learn to sound like they do (over a couple of days this summer I taught my niece Kelsey the magic of a Mourning Dove coo and a rooster cock-a-doodle-doo). How do you engage with those whose joie d' vivre is so palpable they almost fill the room? Unprompted smiles breaking across your face just being with them? Other than having mud slathered on your face at a spa when was the last time you made a mud pie with your kids, rather than worrying about them tracking mud into the house? Or something perhaps more purposeful such as digging in the Earth to plant a tree or put in a whole garden—rather than hiring someone to do it for you?

Watch teenagers hang, listening to music, talking—the dynamic can be riveting and makes you recall who you were at 17 or 19, remember that person? My eyes fill with joyful tears at their exquisite youthful beauty, the whole world waiting for them to conquer, the infinite which lay before them on roads yet unimagined or travelled. John Mellencamp's "Jack & Diane ©" plays in my head the poignant refrain resonates more completely than I imagined could be possible; yes, oh do, '*Hold on to 16 as long as you can, changes come along real soon, make us women and men.*'

How do you see your life? Is abundance the defining word? Or somehow sorely lacking? Just as you can re-program your brain to be a morning person (yes, it takes some effort) according to some scientific evidence you can actually re-wire yourself to be happy, healthy, chronically optimistic, peaceful and free of physical pain as Epernicus taught.

The scope of possibilities to transform our lives begins with love, loving kindness, passion, tenderness, understanding, commitment, responsibility, integrity, grace and the joy I can only describe as being inherent in small children but which society leeches out of so many of us by the time we barely reach adolescence. With all these, taken even in small measure, the purest element of our human essence truly seeks our light to shine forth. The truly beautiful thing about this is that no matter how damaged we might have become on our way to adulthood we have the ability to heal, grow stronger, softer (as my friend Jenn says 'resilient') again.

I started a business in a foreign country (with no seed capital or investors) designed to preserve traditional skills, positively impact local economies leveraging a 'Fair Trade on steroids meets bespoke luxury' business model—that scared me absolutely senseless. The resulting income from a global marketplace and validation through earned media for 85 year old hand-knitters in publications such as *The Economist*,© *The Times of London*© and Forbes.com© has been the most rewarding communications effort of my career. We have developed trade relationships which have positively impacted more individuals economically than I could have imagined. I realise that not everyone will consider starting a business in another country. I know I am oversimplifying but why remain static (and perhaps thoroughly miserable) when life offers such infinite possibilities for experiencing a real joy which resonates with you and you alone?

If life is a glass then it should never be half empty but always at least half full. This applies especially when your beloved vintage Saab© convertible needs quad digits of repairs and there's exactly $33 in your wallet and no open credit on your plastic—at least you were a mere 3 miles from your garage and not alone on a cross country road trip. See how being grateful shifts the impact of the repair bill?

I vividly recall my maternal grandmother, Vera Viola Noyes, telling me on the day of her 84th birthday, "I don't know where all the years went. In my head I am still nineteen." Perhaps the genetic code of her mother (according to family legend my great grandmother ran away and joined the circus), as passed onto me, is the reason I see possibilities looming large before me instead of limitations. Why I believe a life well lived is about drinking, inhaling, experiencing passionately, being deeply aware of pleasure, loving yourself and those around you with every fiber of your being and eating really good chocolate (more on that later) along the way. Why, despite arthritis announcing its presence in my hands each time the barometric pressure changes, I rejoice in opportunities to expand my physical horizons, in addition to those mental and emotional which pique my interest. I am not the only one.

On 25 July 2011 Julie Armstrong arrived at the base of her first mountain with her best friend of more than 30 years. Mount Kilimanjaro for her is a beacon to a life well lived. I think she's nuts. She's used her knitting money (Julie was one of the 35 hand-knitters that supported a collaboration of my Edinburgh based company, Thistle & Broom, and Clarks Originals© for their AW11/12 ladies collection) to purchase her Shewee,© yes, it is exactly what you think it is and no, I don't care to ever need try one out!, down parka, special sunglasses et al.

Diana Nyad, age 61, whose initial freeze frame of celebrity came more than 30 years ago when she swam around the island of Manhattan didn't want to live the remainder of her life thinking "what if?" Instead she decided "large" was the word she wanted to describe her time on Earth so, she got back in the water. In the summer of 2011 Diana attempted to swim non-stop for at least 60 hours in the open water, unprotected (no shark cage, no touching the support boat, just her goggles, bathing suit and swim cap) for a 103 miles, not factoring the impact of the Gulf Stream carrying her further east and having to swim back, from Havana, Cuba to Key West, Florida. As she was about to commence her swim she told CNN,[©] "It's not about sports. It's about hope." Yes, 29 hours in, halfway to Florida, she had to quit because of the excruciating pain in her shoulder, a debilitating attack of asthma and countless Jelly-fish stings but she had tried, saying, "The swim was in me, the conditions weren't right."

My lifeguard friend Kyle Kraeger has a 93 year old (or rather young) great, grandfather. He still lives alone, still drives. He comes together for dinner every Sunday night with his children, grandchildren and great grandchildren. Recently Grandpa Robert (Stark) fell asleep during this weekly family event. This is evidently somewhat unusual given his extremely vigorous being. When he woke he was asked if he felt okay. Turns out he'd been chopping cord wood for 3 hours earlier in the day. Three hours of swinging an axe in 80+ degree weather in your nineties? How amazing! His son-in-law, age 70, recently passed for the husband of his granddaughter (absent because she was competing in a Muscleman competition—½ of a Triathlon) at the place where three generations normally stop for breakfast on their weekly bike rides of 30 miles. My own family has nothing in common with the Stark-Kraeger clan's fountain of youth but I try to convey a similar passion for life to my nieces and nephew.

Mary Granville Pendarves Delany (1700–1788) was married off at 16 to improve her family's fortunes, widowed at 25 and, finally, remarried for love in her forties. It was only following the protracted mourning of the death of both her sister and her beloved second husband of twenty-three years that she began, at age 72, what became a glorious legacy for the rest of us to enjoy. In a mixed-media collage art-form now commonly known as *Flora Delanica*, which can be found in the British Museum in London, Mrs Delany painstakingly developed some 985 botanically correct 'cut paper flowers.' She labored for a decade before her eyesight and health precluded the completion her stated goal of 1000 examples. Breath-taking is only a merely adequate word to describe the beauty and the astonishing effort involved.

What's clear about each of these individuals, and perhaps their families, is that physical and creative challenges did not cease to be part of their reality in their twenties or thirties. Play is not only for little kids, and it's not so much about what you do but the passion and joy you are capable of putting into the activity.

I don't believe that staying relevant into your nineties (or sixties) is simply about physical fitness (although Mrs Delany was evidently an avid walker) it's also about keeping your brain engaged. The challenge of learning something new, in any environment is critical to the quality of our lives.

Admittedly I haven't ever given much thought about my paternal grandfather in this context. He spent more of my life in a nursing home than playing with me yet still I know I was the apple of his eye. A series of mini-strokes and mild heart-attacks left him in a wheel chair before I was six; he died when I was twelve. More than 40 years on I can recall the smell of that nursing home, especially the smell of disinfectant and what I can only describe as 'old people waiting to die.' I simply tear up at the contrast between my own grandfather and Kyle's great-Grandpa Robert. With friends' parents in their eighties now in assisted living facilities I look back on my Grandpa's life as it intersected with my own and I realise just how heart-breaking it was for a man in his fifties to 'live' like this.

So, don't. Right now, change something about your perspective. Challenge yourself mentally or physically; something small at first, then increasing larger. If you've never travelled outside of a 100 mile radius of the town you were born plan a weekend trip that is 200 miles away. Read a book about a topic in which you have interest but you believe to be above your head—it probably isn't and even if it is look up the words you don't understand. Learning can be as small as a single new word each day. Take up calligraphy or painting or learn to ice skate—even if you are 75.

My next challenge is to renew, and then subsequently expand my long dormant French language skills. Why? Maybe because it's insufficient for me to read only a wine label or menu to understand 'what's inside' or to know what the map of France looks like both today as when historically it wasn't France per se and Helen of Aquitaine was being pursued by Henry IV (or was it the other way around?). Okay, it's also because I have never owned a home of my own—ever. And I fully expect to realise this important first, and likely last, purchase will be someplace between Languedoc and Provence-Alpes. As my friend Philippe cannot rescue me even with his native skills (his forte is not in dealing with electricians and plumbers and land surveyors but in selecting wines to cellar) I will be dealing with everyone from the bankers and solicitors to the green grocer on my own.

To do so effectively and efficiently also means being respectful, and not coming across as some 'entitled, ugly American' expecting the residents of France to speak English. I hope my efforts are worthy of this ancient beautiful language.

2
doesn't it smell like a fish?

The truth is we are ALL very funny, even more so when we are operating within a ridiculous place of seriousness. The little idiosyncrasies which define us would make us verbal cannon fodder and life miserable if not for the human capacity to laugh at ourselves, the process of learning this is not easy but it is necessary. Some of us are very funny simply being absolutely serious as evident in the long history of the 'straight man.' Others can bring the house down with a cleverly turned phrase, or self-deprecating humour. But to me one of the greatest things about being a modern day Pollyanna or Rebecca of Sunnybrook Farm (read incredibly naïve with a joy for life), maintaining the ability to still blush with youthful integrity is being called out and then truly recognizing how silly my outward appearance, words or behaviour can be.

I spent three months, virtually every day, sitting on the pool deck of my health club writing. I am still able, as my third grade teacher Mrs Mason wrote on one of my report cards to "work(s) well alone." So truly it never occurred to me that if I was only marginally aware of the goings on around me why my presence should be noticed by anyone lounging by the pool or playing with their kids in the water. It was with surprise and hilarity that I was called on my eccentricities by a local restaurateur who happens to be a client of my girlfriend Jenn. According to Joe I would sit there typing away in beat with the music (this I know and admit to) an invisible bubble around me (obviously not tinted), entirely lost in the capturing of my thoughts and words. Evidently, I have the habit of reading slightly aloud, laughing to myself (likely text or emails coming in) and then with some level of animation return to my typing. Joe tells this with mirth. Jenn splits her sides. The colour rises in my face then flushes my neck on downward, which, of course, only makes Joe and Jenn laugh harder and me join their revelry.

My delightful nephew, Michael Logan, learned to swim at his parents' country club pool, and, as such, he was conditioned early on to use the bathroom as might be necessary. Of course with a pool in his own wooded backyard the rules changed a little. Rather than traipse wet through the house he'd been given permission to simply 'pee in the bushes.' As a Montessori Pre-K student some modification was going to be necessary. Among his promises before leaving for school each day now include, "Mommy, I promise not to pee in the grass."

Back in the summer of 2004 I was very graciously invited to come spend the afternoon of the 4th of July with my boss Ann and her family. It was entirely reasonable to assume that I would be driving to their home—but I wasn't, I was going to ride my bike primarily because I didn't own a car at the time. The thing about this isn't the bike ride but its timing and distance. To arrive at 2PM as expected meant leaving by 11:30. My apartment was just slightly higher than sea level—the street rising from the pier on about a 35% grade plus my second story loft space above art gallery bringing the total to perhaps 100 feet above sea level. Whereas Ann's family lived inland essentially sixteen miles straight UP hill! Midday, July Fourth, heat and humidity as only Connecticut can produce, me and my bike. The directions were fine. I had plenty of fluids to make the ride. I arrived on time asking only if I could get cleaned up. I had brought soap, a washcloth, a fresh shirt, deodorant and did the best I could to mitigate the combined effects of weather and exertion on my personal hygiene in their powder room. Late in the afternoon as we sit down to eat Ann's eldest daughter (then in high school) sitting near me says, "Mom? It smells a little like dead fish in here." To which I blushed but responded, "Um, Kate that would be me." There's a kind of stunned, embarrassed silence all around and then as I laugh, we all do—wildly.

15

I can be pretty amusing especially when I am not trying to be, or when it suddenly dawns on me I have said something outrageous with a double meaning and I didn't 'get it' until perhaps 30 seconds later. I have my former husband to thank for teaching me to laugh at myself, I admit before I fell in love with him I was 'way too serious' about absolutely everything. Stephen had an astonishing gift for lightening my actions with gentle humour directed squarely at me.

Despite its being Scotland's capital, its UNESCO status and a global tourist destination Edinburgh remains small and accessible in a way New York, Paris and Berlin can never be. Visiting for the very first time I repeatedly ran into a group of five Royal Scots Dragoon Guards. The gentlemen—Monty, Ross, Dean, Kevin and Brian—and they all truly were, resplendent in their formal dress, beribboned, silver chain mail epaulets, and yes, spurs. Save for one. As they walked away from our second encounter having just graciously posed for a picture with me I noticed that Dean wasn't wearing any and said as much, "Oh, you poor dear man, you are spur less." Truly, incredible as it might seem that I was 40 years old, I didn't understand what the ensuing hysterics and ribbing being doled out where about. But, just as in chemistry and physics for every action there is a like reaction, every wrong must be somehow righted. Three hours later I walked into Deacon Brodie's (a Royal Mile fixture) to await friends for dinner and ran smack dab into the guys for a third time. I had hoped that my comment had been lost to the pitchers of beer and Whisky since our last parting but if it had it now began anew, and Dean had had plenty of time to come up with clever repartee. I offered to buy him a drink to apologise, he rejected my hospitality but offered his own and then . . . took my hand put it high up on his (lovely, well-muscled) thigh, covering it with his own to keep mine in place and pressed down saying, 'when you have these to guide a mare you don't need spurs.' Oh. My. Goodness. For a woman long out of teenage years I blush remarkably easily, no doubt at this moment more boldly than perhaps humanly possible, accompanied by a great deal of laughter all around.

My girlfriend Mia was en route to a wedding with her boyfriend. On a shuttle flight with only one other passenger, seemingly the photographer, she was chatting about the mouthful of consonants which the groom's last name was and speculated aloud how much more sense it made for the groom to take his bride's name of Logan. She decided to engage the photographer on the mystery of Eastern European surnames and presumably secure his approval of her theory. He replied that he didn't think the name was very difficult as it was his own—the photographer was actually the father of the groom.

So, when was the last time you had a good belly laugh at your own expense at some distinctive foible of yours? Try it. Don't take yourself so seriously. Life is just too short.

18 • all that i need

3 duncan

It was midday on the Saturday of Memorial Day weekend 2004. I was enjoying a day trip to Westport, Connecticut, with Patricia, a very dear girlfriend from college. The sky was blue, the sun out, flags decorated every light pole and the entire bridge running through town heading down Connecticut's Gold Coast toward Greenwich, and we were walking up Main Street to get an iced coffee for Patricia. When I saw him, I stopped dead in my tracks. Duncan is tangible evidence of the very real power which the spoken word can sometimes have. If you have even an inkling of belief in the power of intention I would caution you to be very specific about your wants, needs and requirements.

He's fast and charms everyone who meets him as well as virtual strangers with his silent *je ne sais quoi*. While it was a 'whoa' kind of love-at-first-sight on my part I think he's grown used to our relationship. He's remarkably high maintenance for middle age requiring the regular ministrations of a half a dozen skilled professionals in three states. If he can know anything at all, it's that his physical needs will be attended to even if it means a level of financial sacrifice which I am often hard put to accommodate. My dearest friends recognise that there might have been more practical choices but freely acknowledge that my identity and his are now inexplicably, and imperfectly, linked. There's a very real truth to their words, "it's hard to imagine you with any other."

As a point of clarity, Duncan is not the man in my life. Rather he is my beloved 1989 Saab 900 Turbo convertible, manual transmission, black with tan leather interior (is there any other combination?) with just under 100,000 miles on his odometer. His story is part of my own and obviously relevant to my life's philosophy.

At the time I met Duncan I had been out of work as a director of marketing communications, largely in the Internet Technology space, for nearly three years. I had held my life together with bits of thread and duct tape, with the help of friends, an amazing ex-husband whose generous spirit and integrity should be the standard for how former spouses interact with their ex's and selling personal possessions on eBay.© There was nothing glamorous about it—it was hard. Many friends expressed wonder that I wasn't sitting on the floor in a corner in a white jacket which buckled in the back, drooling on myself. The thought had crossed my mind more than once.

The weekend started with a rental car for which I really had no idea how I was going to pay when the bill came due, a 380 mile one way trip for a 3PM interview on the Friday afternoon of a holiday weekend, and a very-necessary-to-land consulting role at Pfizer's Global Research and Development Headquarters.

In 1998 I had the good fortune to land a position with an emerging technology company called CertCo, LLC. I had worked every angle and connection imaginable for three months, ultimately getting in the door through 'a friend of a friend' at Banker's Trust

Venture Capital and claiming the position as my own just as my unemployment was about to run out. I was the primary point of contact for launching the consortia of international commercial banks and their technology partner's (CertCo) identity platform named on my watch as Identrust. Six years later Pfizer was about to apply the same business model and technology to create a uniform identity platform which would reduce its environmental impact and improve efficiencies across seven business units and impact 250,000 people on a global basis.

At the time I was not aware I was 'connected' to anyone at Pfizer to help make this happen. Four weeks before the invoice for legal services and incorporation for Thistle & Broom© had come in for over £900 and I looked at my ceiling and said out-loud "God, I have followed all your messages to bring to this point. But now, if you really want me to do this, I need a job."

A week later, out-of-the-blue, I received a phone call from the man who had inherited my job with Identrust in 2001. Paul said, "I am in the car with the hiring manager at Pfizer. You might be the only communications person on the planet who could walk into this job. No one in the role has lasted more than three weeks so I wouldn't relocate. The contract is set up on renewable three month terms. Are you available? Are you interested? Name your price." Obviously the answer was yes to the first two questions but I had never done any Fortune 50 consulting before—how do you price your expertise within a very narrow technology and business model for a very big company and not look seriously stupid?

So I drove to New London, CT, and got through the interview just fine (Scott, the hiring manager—literally a rocket scientist—was great, less so his boss David who struck me as one of those people promoted along the way to get him actually out of the way) but then it's out of my hands. There's no way I can physically turn the car around, my sciatica was acting up, and drive back 380 miles to return the car before Enterprise© closed. So in a manner of speaking I was stuck with the rental, unlimited mileage across New England, for the weekend.

Patricia is putting me up at her place near Litchfield; I plan to stop to prowl through its antique shops 'sightseeing' Sunday on my return trip. So I drive the two hours north and west of New London to her place.

We have a lovely evening, pack provisions and agree that stopping at (yum) Trader Joe's© makes sense to fill out our planned picnic.

En route Patricia says, 'If you land the job at Pfizer you can afford to buy any car you want.'

My reply is totally unrealistic but pretty specific. "Yeah, I know. Honestly all I really want is a pre-GM,© late model Saab© convertible. A five speed, preferably black with a tan leather interior, low mileage, no rust and never been in an accident."

Less than two hours later, sitting in the public parking lot on Main Street Westport with an ugly neon orange For Sale sign in the window **E-V-E-R-Y-T-H-I-N-G** I had expressed that I wanted in my 'next car' was sitting in front of me. I got down on the ground to check the under-carriage (be assured if you've never been to Westport this kind of behaviour is frowned upon) the frame is straight and, as far as I can tell, the car is completely rust free. I write down the VIN to do a CarFax© check, note the phone number and because I don't know if the Pfizer job is mine or not I do nothing further. Two weeks pass and phone calls are being made back and forth negotiating start dates and money, feeling a little more confident about the future I called about the car. I knew how little I could live on and still be 'happy' (the answer is virtually nothing!) but making Thistle & Broom a reality was going to take serious money and though my work place ultimately was less than 2 miles from the apartment I rented, a car for grocery shopping was going to be very necessary—I just failed to adequately judge the cost of owning Duncan. The wife answers the phone, can't recall the car even being out of the garage over the last month and her husband had pulled the ad from the paper. When I tell her when and where I saw it she's astonished (me too) as it turns out that the car and I shared this finite block of hour and a half of time in Westport. Yes, it's still for sale, she'll have her husband call me back. I am so grateful for Scott's, and in turn David's boss Ann being from Rochester, NY. Ann seeing my resume with a Rochester address weeks before, had said something to the effect of 'Hello? Rochester? Why haven't we spoken to this woman?' It's largely because of Ann that I was on-boarded in record time—under three weeks—that Thistle & Broom exists and Duncan is mine. Thanks so much, still, Ann!

Cars, just as lovers, can be equally unresponsive to someone other than their master or mistress—no dominatrix reference intended. The clutch synchronisation on most manual transmissions somehow becomes an extension of the cars' primary driver. As I had to have the transmission and clutch replaced within a month of taking possession, Duncan's is no exception. Aside from the nuances of his shifting he developed a tendency to stall if he got too warm or, more specifically, if it was too warm outside and he also got too warm—I can't recall if it was the thermostat or rheostat. How we avoided any, let alone a serious, accident is absolutely beyond comprehension. Until I could afford to have the problem diagnosed and subsequently fixed, I developed an unimagined level of patience for this cloying behaviour because I don't do well in the heat either. Surely his Swedish origins deserved a little tolerance on my part since he wasn't built to positively respond to the heat wave which poured over the Tri-State area and New England during the summer of 2006.

I had to be in Scotland for an extended period of time. My friend Alan agreed to collect and park him someplace inexpensive until he could be driven out to the North Fork of Long Island where I was living in Alan's deceased mother's senior citizens community (minimum age requirement 55 unless staying as a guest, tongues evidently wagged for which I was blissfully unaware until Alan told me some four years later). Duncan was left in a mid-town Manhattan garage not far from Alan's office. Despite being educated in posh English schools by his Scottish parents and a 'serious' businessman, Alan has come to have some level of pleasurable regard for my considerable idiosyncrasies and maintains particular good humour about Duncan—although I am quite certain he's never named a vehicle he has driven in his entire life. To this day he remains the only person other than me or one of his mechanics to ever drive Duncan—mind you not without slapstick humourous results, which five years on still make me laugh so hard as to prevent me from catching my breath. In fairness Alan did indicate his ability to drive a standard transmission. Still, I think his middle name should be 'chivalry.'

I should share, for those unfamiliar with pre-GM Saabs or the history of the company in the first instance, that the company tag line is *Born of Jets.*™ The instrument panels are very much like that of a single engine airplane (I only know that because I was terrified of turning 30 and took one up ONCE to get over both fears) laid out neatly in front of you and remarkably intuitive. The ignition on Duncan sits on the floor console (no drag on the ignition switch from too many keys on a key ring) between the driver and passenger seat, behind the stick and in front of the hand brake and the electronic controls for the windows. But in a dark garage, at the end of the day, who has time to learn this when dozens of impatient New Yorkers are behind you wanting to get home to Greenwich or out to The Hamptons? As the car was running there was little issue about this lack of familiarity and Alan headed out into the mass of midtown Manhattan humanity. His tetchy habit of stalling when warm kicked in sooner than 'normal' at the rather inopportune narrowing of 66th Street at Central Park as Alan attempted to exit the city toward Merrimac. It is an unenviable position, Friday evening Manhattan rush hour stalled in a car and you don't know where the ignition is so you can restart the car again. Suffice to say Alan and Duncan's Paso Doble was not stellar and though Alan prevailed he wanted to crawl under a rock from embarrassment. I can only imagine Alan's perfect courtly behaviour almost wishing Duncan to assume human form at the conclusion of this drive so he might issue a challenge to dual to gain his satisfaction.

Seven years into our 'partnership,' only three of which I have generated a regular paycheck, maintenance costs related to oil changes, tires, system flushes and the occasional belts notwithstanding, Duncan has had at minimum: a new head gasket, transmission and clutch, new exhaust system, new water pump, modified AC unit and new compressor and relay switch, driver, passenger and windshield glass replaced, brakes and rotor pads (his were original and finally seized up), a new ragtop and then, later, because something was wrong with the headliner a new one of those, new radiator, not one but two alternators and, of course, two batteries, a duplicate set of original issue alloy rims (because, the price for four was less than one would have been and the rubber was still in great shape), exhaustive work to ensure directional signals worked and then dashboard viewing could take place. A new "old" replacement passenger door and hood have been located to combat the small amounts of rust suddenly appearing on his 24 year old body. He leaks like a sieve when you go through a car wash, requiring his own set of towels ever present in the trunk to block water, soap and fluffy blue and pink wax from coming in the tiniest gap in the driver's side window and covering me. I am probably the only straight woman on the planet that currently has a 'just in case' brand new clutch sitting on her kitchen floor next to the onion basket under the chrome cart holding her cookware. I view the accompanying stack of receipts for Duncan's 'spa treatments' as my car payments and the related expense ensures that he will be the last car I ever drive. I humbly attribute my affection for driving Duncan to the fact that one of the most extraordinary female actresses ever to grace the screen, Katherine Hepburn, drove her own stick shift Saab up until almost her passing.

There's two ways of looking at my relationship with Duncan, and, frankly quite equally, for coping with the many frustrations life can offer.

First, as with any relationship, there is some kind of cost/benefit ratio we constantly subconsciously matrix. If, at any time, the pleasure/joy/reward is mitigated by the pain/expense we can (and should) simply walk away.

Secondly, I accept responsibility for every one of my choices. Collectively we have gotten far too good at blaming someone else for the choices we make around everything from our expanding waistlines to our national debt.

No one forced this car on me or the related, and sometimes crazy, costs of ownership. I brought this fully upon myself as much by specifically stating the precise car I desired to own but for also not stating that I wanted a mechanically sound car and being too stubborn to walk away from him. I am not proud to admit that there is also my ego involved; my friend Richard once told me I looked amazing behind his wheel, top down, music blaring, my nieces boyfriends comment that 'your aunt drives the coolest car ever,' occasionally someone (in any number of cities) chases me down and begs me to take their card should I ever decide to sell. Duncan has inspired the trade-in of a much newer, mechanically sound Mazda© to purchase one of his Saab cousins—a 2000 dark grey sedan now named Kyle. A couple of times the drive-thru attendant has asked me a hundred questions before my order arrived because he's 17 and never seen a 1989 anything car let alone likely the best looking year of production Saab ever manufactured.

A vintage car of any kind is a purse emptying folly much like restoring an old house; what joy is mine to own something so utterly irresponsible? At the end of the day I could drive something 'reliable' but what fun would that be?

4 when did you become a headbanger?

More than anything else I believe in making memories.

The ordinary should be liberally sprinkled with Tinkerbelle's faery dust and the contents of Mary Poppins© carpet bag because most of us do not possess Harry Potter's© friend Hermione's time-turner to make room for more in our day, nor do we get a 'do-over.'

When I started writing this book my lifeguard friends would tune Pandora to Coldplay or Adele or some dance techno compilation so I could type in synch with the beat of the music. Forever, I will associate children's laughter, their doing cannonballs into the pool, wet flip-flops on concrete and the sounds of Katy Perry or Florence and The Machine with writing the first 100 pages of **All That I Need**.

One of my most favourite memories is shared with my nieces Kate and Julia, and their friends Katie Teren and Tori Khalil the day before Christmas of 2004. I had arrived back in Rochester, NY for the holidays from Connecticut where I was living. I had my vintage Saab convertible a couple months at that point which my nieces had not yet seen. I wanted them to understand that the magic of driving with the top down is not limited to summertime, or daylight.

Who wants to go for a ride in Duncan?

We have to take turns because there are only three passenger seats. I put the top down, turn the heat up, give the girls wool blankets to tuck in around them and set off in a 'one horse open sleigh.' Soon we've got the stereo as loud as it will go, and we're belting out Christmas carols at the top of our lungs on a star-filled 19 degree (plus the wind chill factor) night. Although the pavement was dry when we set out, snowflakes the size of cornflakes commenced swirling around us almost magically as Bing Crosby sang White Christmas.© My friend Dan comments at Christmas Day dinner that he'd seen some 'crazy person driving their Saab convertible around with the top down on Christmas Eve, and then realised—'HEY! I know that crazy person.' Same dinner my amazing, astonishing niece Kate is sitting next to me, announces, "Aunt Terri? You are never going to be old like my Nana are you?" Inside I am glowing, but OHGAWD, her Nana is opposite me. How cool is it to be a couple years younger than her mom and have this child, so dear to my heart, somehow separate me from those growing old (and older) around her?

Six Christmas seasons later my nieces' social schedules are far too busy with their friends, and boyfriends, I am delighted to comply with a nearly begging request to take the forty-something sister of a dear girlfriend's fiancé out for a ride in Duncan. The snow is deep, the air cold, the Christmas Eve sky midnight blue, a nearby bonfire sends ancient burning wood smells and sparks to the heavens beckoning both Divine and our own personal rebirth and, yes, Santa too! Wendy, wearing the über-cool leather jacket her brother

Chris has just given her for Christmas, is ebullient with the prospect. Her delighted laughter rings out as I put his top down, I think she figured we would go for conventional?, her laughter grows louder as the stereo is turned on to the local classic rock station. We take off, shifting easily up to 5th in the length of the rural road and into the city. 10 months later Wendy can't believe when I share that I am including her moment with Duncan in this chapter. "I thought that what you did was only special to me." No Wendy, bringing other people joy also makes a memory for me.

Recently I picked up my girlfriend Jenn's daughter and a friend of hers, both 14, to drive down to the family's lake house. I freely admit that 7 out of 10 times my taste in music is much like that of a teenage boy; I do not however decorate my home with metal hair band posters from the 1970's. There is no match for the exhilaration I feel driving (fast) on the highway, top down, the little dial turned as far up as possible, *American Woman* screaming from my speakers. People stare—or they absolutely get it and give me a thumb's up. It strikes me as a most important imperative of my life to transfer this ability to drive well concurrently with rocking it out. The girls loaded in, seat belts on, I think I shocked them with 'just how loud' was permissible in my car. In two seconds they are singing, dancing in their seats and having a blast. The deal is that while I enjoy contemporary pop rock on a day such as this every fifth song must be something from 1969 to 1983.

Jenn manages to catch-up a half hour later and pulls ahead of me so I know where we're going. We stop for fresh corn. As Jenn gets out of her Audi she's conveying her rant about 'the obnoxious teenagers playing their car stereo too loud' and how her daughter Hannah (Indigo Child, age 10) says "Mom . . ." assuming Mom will understand precisely what she means by 'Mom.' This goes back and forth three or four rounds with Jenn replying "what Hannah?" until Hannah, knowing look plastered across her face like mom is an idiot, finally says, "Mom. It's Teresa." For her it is the most natural thing in the universe for her esoteric philosopher mother to have a renegade friend with a penchant for acting like a teenager.

My ex-husband has the distinction for calling me out on 'this behaviour' a couple years after we divorced and the title of this chapter. When, in getting into my car to drive someplace together the stereo and the engine conjoined someplace in the neighbourhood of 80 decibels cranking out Michael Bolton singing "The Hunger,©" he said, "Terri, when did you become a headbanger?" (Michael Bolton head-banger music? Maybe when his hair band Blackjack toured with Ozzy Osbourne, but really, wicked grin, truly I am NOT.)

Can rock music really accomplish so much? Well, no, not exactly. My love of music transcends genre. The one universally applicable characteristic it must have—aside from being the perfect example of whatever it is, Baroque Chamber and Led Zeppelin alike—is to be played LOUD! I want to feel music resonate in my bones, to make my blood pulse with echoing reverberations, to make my body feel like a tuning fork.

I was living in Boston in the late 1990's, blessed with a remarkable circle of friends who were multi-lingual, very cultured and largely European. To put the intelligence of this group into perspective, one German woman casually read Dante's *Inferno* in the original Italian for fun. No matter how much confidence I might possess about the breadth of my knowledge I often felt (seriously) lacking in their collective presence. I was about to turn 39. It was doubtful my French would ever allow me to read Voltaire's *Candide* in the original. Though I had certainly read the plot lines for a great many operas and listened as someone dying of thirst might to NPRs *Live from the Met* broadcasts, my only live operatic experience to date had been an-hour-before-performance purchase of Wagner's den Tannhäuser at the Deutsche Oper Berliner the year before. No matter how incredible the music that night (and, IT WAS EXTRAORDINARY) somehow in wearing jeans and a navy jacket to the performance diminished the experience because I was self-conscious about my attire. For these and a thousand other reasons turning 39 was making me feel like so much of my life was left undone.

I remain forever in debt to Dr Gerold & Mrs Sissi Ebenbischler of Wien, Austria for the most remarkable way to experience a live operatic performance. Gerold was on an exchange residency in sports medicine with University of Boston and was part of my circle of friends. In mentioning my intention to travel to Vienna and Budapest in February Gerold invited me to stay with he and his wife and son. In expressing my desire to attend the Vienna State Opera, Sissi had a girlfriend who had been on the women's committee for over 20 years who could help with my ticket, how much did I want to spend? Just as attending your first major league baseball game would unthinkable to sit in the grandstand, if you are going to travel more than 4000 miles and spend nearly 10 hours in a plane seat to see a live opera then the cost of the ticket should not be a consideration. I put a $200 USD threshold on the cost and hoped for the best.

Regardless of where I was going to sit there was no way I was going to attend a second opera in jeans, or a short dress for that matter. This was my birthday and even if I was spending it alone I wanted it to be exponentially memorable.

So, regardless of the price, wearing off the rack (when your grandmother was a gifted seamstress), was never going to be an option. Shortly after booking the plane tickets I got very lucky in a vintage shop on Charles Street in finding a bolt of emerald green silk satin—thick, luscious stuff. I had a princess seamed, flared from the waist to the mermaid hem, self-fabric buttoned down the front to the knee, just slightly-off-the-edge-of-the-shoulder gown made along with a bespoke corset made to wear under it. When it was finished, I felt like a goddess in it. Though I was only going to the opera I felt like I was 'attending the ball.'

The night of the opera—everything hoped, imagined and more becomes my reality; drinking Champagne from glass flutes in the lobby, ascending the grand gas-lit staircase, the sound of the silk of my skirt across the marble, the opulence of my seat which turns out to be in the president of Austria's box. No waaaay! Random bows glide across strings. Lights down. The orchestra tunes, swells of violins lift playing the overture of Il Trovatore; a lucky coincidence given my affinity for the Middle Ages. The gentleman sitting next to me is in white tie and tails, sashed, beribboned and adorned with gold enamelled and jewel encrusted state honours and turns out to be a Bratislavan diplomat—endless kindness in lending me his opera glasses. Assuming I was wearing a glass slipper this night, for one night, all things are possible—sadly, the glass slippers were sold out in my size.

At the opposite end of the cultural music spectrum Crosby, Still and Nash. My then colleague Henry, whose best buddy ditched him at the last minute, invited me to join him. I was sitting in the waterfront pavilion in Boston 11 rows from the stage. CSN's considerably over middle age bodies belay the still strong harmonies of their voices. As the audience is largely the Woodstock Generation, I am struck by how mellow they all are. I am absolutely the youngest person in the audience, my affinity for CSN honed in the 7th grade in my girlfriend Eden's basement with her parents' albums. The rhythms swell inside me and soon I was standing on my chair, dancing. Not long after I was tying my white blouse into a midi because there wasn't an ounce of air moving under the canvas and sweat was pouring off me. I am sure Henry both wanted to die of embarrassment and join me—not a single other person moves from their seat. What happened to these children of The Summer of Love?

The year of my separation, when I worked for Turner Broadcasting, I lived in very likely the safest neighbourhood soon–to-be-single straight woman could; within a twenties vintage red brick apartment building located at 12th NE in Midtown Atlanta overlooking Piedmont Park. My across the hallway neighbour was a gay hairdresser named Chaz Montgomery, downstairs a gay flight attendant and his roommate (not partner). My sexuality was pegged in under two minutes, it took me a little longer to figure out the lay-of-the-land as it were—needless to say the boys had a ball with my naïveté.

One memorable night I was transformed into a living, breathing Barbie doll. Chaz came over to ransack my closet and drawers to select my wardrobe for the evening deciding upon a pair of cuffed white cotton Bermuda's, navy and white spectator lace-ups, a navy double breasted cotton jacket and a blue lace bra. He slicked my hair down, with a goo that later took four washings get out, and tiger braided it tightly against my scalp. Eight of us headed to a club called Petrus located within a fabulous Reconstruction-era mansion complete with a reflecting pool and three fountains in the courtyard. No matter how many dance floors (or bar tops) I had spent time on in the late 70's and early 80's I have to admit that as I turned 30 I never expected to find myself in a similar position, wearing only my bra and shorts, on top of a 10' tall speaker, Voguing. Thanks Madonna!

Nina Kraus, director of the auditory Neuroscience Laboratory at Northwestern University says, "If you spend a lot of your life interacting with sound in an active manner, then your nervous system has made lots of sound-to-meaning connections." Those efforts can theoretically strengthen your auditory system. I don't know if this applies only to playing an instrument or if listening counts, but surely the sound track of our lives plays a critical role in assuring that years on we're transported back to something wonderful.

If you have been living with the volume turned down, not just on the music but how you relate to it, how you live your life, I can't encourage you enough to let it rip!

5 ticket to ride

Sometime during my senior year in high school I recall being in a Pizza Hut© grabbing a quick meal between my job at the local wallpaper and paint store and before heading to my job as a tour guide in Niagara Falls. Two booths in front of mine, on the other side of the restaurant, was a family with a young man with Cerebral Palsy. His family fully engaged amongst themselves but he was left alone within the banter and conviviality. Something was visibly distressing him but absolutely no one within his family paid the slightest attention nor made any effort to soothe the problem. When I got to my car I wept bitter, angry tears.

The experience never really left me but it (sort of) came rushing back to me thirty plus years later one afternoon when out for a 'progressive lunch' with my girlfriend Sue. We had thoroughly enjoyed these miraculous steamed pork buns (Hoisin sauce, chopped peanuts, scallions, grilled pork belly—sigh) in one restaurant and then headed down the street to a second restaurant for Hot & Sour soup and another appetizer to complete our meal. A woman in a (non-motorized) wheelchair sat alone at the table next to ours. We were still eating when she finished her lunch and was helped outside to the sidewalk. Restaurant #2 was situated a bit down from the highest elevation of the street—all up-hill for this grey haired lady. She was still working her way home trying to cross the busy main thoroughfare when we were heading back to the car. She was stuck in the midst of the marked crosswalk of four lanes, with traffic unyielding. It was terrifying to even watch, I can't imagine sitting there as she did so vulnerable. Finally the driver on the far side stopped for her—Sue and I both let out an audible sigh of relief. I begged Sue to take my wallet and dashed across the street. She said she'd circle the block and come get me.

I apologized in advance to the woman. Said no matter how strong her arms were if she was okay with some help I would like to make sure she got up the hill and home okay. So we chatted about the food at the restaurant and I pushed. And it struck me, able bodied that I am, what little effort it took to make a difference—a tiny measure of treating another human being as I would hope I would be treated if it had been me struggling with a steep grade and an uneven city sidewalk. Her liberty, despite its difficulties, with the wind blowing sweet end-of-summer freshness, satiated with wonderful Asian fusion cooking was complemented less than five minutes later when Sue and I stopped to observe a parking lot temporarily converted into two Cycle Polo grounds.

How a pair of wheels can provide such varying degrees of pleasure and frustration startled my awareness. Six tattooed, often dreadlocked, pierced, t-shirted, helmeted, shin-pad protected polo players on their bikes manoeuvring with insane accuracy within a tiny particle board defined surround. Men and women alike, as polo had been chronicled by Ferdowsi, the 9th century Persian poet and writer of Shahnameh (The Epic of Kings), played. The game of polo, played since at least the 5th century BCE in Persia (now Iran), was originally training for elite guards and battlefield preparation sometimes fielding as many as a 100 players to a side. While I have attended the Champagne-fueled polo matches as can be found in Far Hills, New Jersey and The Hamptons this plebeian adaption of the Game of Kings, though vastly different, was just as much fun to watch. Evidently there is something called Traditional Cycle Polo, developed by an Irishman named Richard J. Mercredy in 1891, which served as point of origination for this variation called Hardcourt Bicycle Polo which sprung out of the Seattle area sometime in the early 2000's. Yes, much like the horse-mounted teams, there is a governing body and tournaments draw participants from around the world. No elegant ladies in posh hats or gents in linen trousers replacing divots between chukkers necessary. Instead a guy runs around with a portable electric drill in hand to make repairs to the pavilion when a bike crashes into the surround taking it down.

Herbert Spencer, who has covered polo for some forty years, wrote in the Financial Times of London: "The delicious adrenaline rush of polo is hard to describe to those who have yet to experience the speed of high-octane ponies, the adulation of spectators and the glamour of the sport."

I have a hard time disagreeing with him. But, when most of those participating in high-goal polo spend upwards of $150,000.00 on a single horse, and a minimum of four are required by each player for a match, is the return-on-investment higher for the likes of Narciso Rodriguez (the astonishing looking player who also models for Ralph Lauren©) or the guy or gal with a DIY mallet and flattened garbage can lids fashioned into spoke covers for their customised bike's wheels?

In May of 2003 I was the sixth playing tag football with the downstairs tenants and their friends (all 18 to 22 year olds). I do have a degree of competency being taught as a little girl by my favourite cousin Tom (played for Woody Hayes at Ohio State) to throw, punt and catch a football making this not much of a stretch. My team had the ball. I went deep to receive and in running backwards failed to take note of the curb behind me. We all heard the noise first and I crumpled to the pavement in excruciating pain—I had torn my Achilles tendon. No health insurance. Really, not good.

It took until October for me to heal sufficiently to walk and then, I overdid it, again. I had stayed off my leg for months and I was nearly stir-crazy from lack of activity. An indie band called Seven Nations I adore was playing at a Celtic festival so off I went to enjoy myself. To their fabulous electric fiddling and piping there were some 500+ people 'just sitting there' listening and a single Down's syndrome young man dancing alone—I couldn't stand it. It flashes in my head that thirty years ago I couldn't, didn't, do anything in that Pizza Hut so I danced with him. It should be noted that while I was tiring the young man clearly was not, so rather than leave him alone I went to reconnoître a replacement for myself. Skipping back to the dance floor with a young miss in tow I thought she mistakenly stepped on my heel; same searing pain, different Achilles tendon. Oh. No. Another four months of inactivity faced me. Actually, it was worse.

Five weeks after my second accident in I managed to land a job interview in Scotland, concern about flying and blood clots forced me to the emergency room. It took two trips as the waiting room was ridiculously full the first trip and the second visit might have ended with self-medicating again had it not been for my redressing and getting up to leave after nearly two hours of waiting on the examining table in little curtained space.

Where are you going?

Home.

You can't leave.

No? Watch me!

But you've filled out the paperwork, you are in our system.

Guess what? Tear it up I am out of here.

We can't do that. If something happens to you . . .

Ah, liability. Tell you what you have exactly five minutes from 'now' to get a Doctor in here or I walk out as I walked in.

The Doctor emerged in three minutes. X-rays followed; with a referral to an Orthopaedic surgeon who was expecting me within the hour close behind.

The Orthopaedic surgeon took one look at the X-rays and ordered an MRI—he frankly couldn't believe I was walking around on the leg so torn.

How did you do this and when?

I tell him the story.

How have you managed to walk?

Barely.

Doctor, I don't have insurance and I am not working at the moment. If we're going to go forward you have to understand it might take me years to pay this debt off.

You let me worry about that.

Back the next day the MRI results in his hands and five weeks into my second healing session I still had a 7mm tear in the Achilles tendon.

You have two choices. What colour cast or we can do out-patient surgery and you will have a scar but you aren't leaving here without my treating you. You will need three casts, one replacing the previous one every fourth week for a total of 12 weeks. He stares at me as I repeat my economic and insured state.

Fine. Candy Apple Red.

For the subsequent cast changes I show up with a loofah, soap, my razor and thick moisturizer and beg to shave my leg. Each time the Physician Assistant balks but the good doctor instructs his PA to bring me a basin of hot water so I can shave my leg. I can't express my happiness! Who gets a Doctor this accommodating?

 43

When the invoice for over $3,000 arrived in the mail it was stamped Paid in Full. Is it possible there really are such people in the world?

My point is this, playing (anything) has very little to do with financial assets and everything to do with attitude. So the lady in the wheel chair, dodging traffic so she can enjoy a plate of General Tso's chicken isn't so very different from the teams whacking a polo mallet from a horse or two wheels or my dancing with the Down's syndrome man. It's about getting out 'there' and living life. Sometimes there's a price to pay, and sometimes there are guardian angels whose appearance helps to make our lives even more precious.

6 i am NOT waiting

A **very long time ago** I learned to be my own best friend. As a child it was a means of self-preservation as there were few kids in our neighbourhood and my parents chose to travel a great deal attending dog shows virtually every weekend during the summer. Now, just because I am not married or currently dating anyone or my friends either aren't available or simply not interested in a particular activity, I am not going to deny myself the pleasure of fully immersing myself in living.

Yes, I dine alone in fine white tablecloth restaurants both domestically and abroad and I never sit in a corner or near the kitchen door—ever.

I enter the rarefied environments of upper Madison Avenue and South Kensington antique shops alone to appreciate, possibly hold but, regrettably, less often than I would like, purchase something truly exquisite.

My 'I-am-not-waiting' excursions have included road trips to see Chris Isaak perform in both Toronto and Boston (many years apart and still no one I knew understood the attraction, which is fair because I really don't get Barry Manilow. If I must explain, aside from the fact that the man is gorgeous, his rockabilly acoustic guitar and vocals make Chris some kind of mental and emotional throw back to my childhood and the collection of 45 RPM Sun Record recordings of my Dad's. Interesting that as I finish writing **All That I Need** Isaak has just released his homage collection of those same Sun artists).

I have packed myself off to France for three day weekends to see special exhibits at the Louvre and Musée National du Moyen Age (in the process delightedly stumbled into a chamber music concert complete with viola de gamba and lute), flown to Utah to ski at the last minute because the fare was dirt cheap and the snow reports promising (standing at the top of those red, orange and maroon striped rocks with the impossibly blue sky above was truly being in God's cathedral). On two separate occasions I have spent two weeks at height of Christmas markets traipsing across Germany, driven to Clayton, NY, to visit the antique boat museum and gone out onto Alexander Bay in a vintage mahogany speed boat and attended lectures on String Theory at MIT. Given my very eclectic interests if I waited on other people to do things with me I would sit home alone for a very long time and become a very dull girl.

What have you left undone because you didn't have someone to do it with? No argument here, yes, the shared experience of doing is very much like a house of mirrors magnifying the original image exponentially. The retelling of the adventure makes the original event potent anew but we don't 'need' others for 'living.' Some variation of 'we come into the world alone and we die alone' is healthy.

And so, on one powder snow filled long weekend as I was painfully going through the separation period leading up to my divorce I packed up my gear and headed, literally, for the hills.

John and his friend Hal (the only reason I even recall his name is I had NEVER met a Hal before nor one since) and three of their mutual friends had converged from all over Canada and the north eastern United States at the same ski resort as I had driven to. These men had known one another for a couple of decades and this was their semi-annual boys' weekend frivolity featuring skiing, great wine (which they brought in by the case), cigars, simple, but fabulous food and a shared condo on the slopes. I wound up on the lift with John given their odd numbers. In discovering that I was skiing alone John and Hal insisted that I join their party to ski for as long as I wanted. As a newly minted and vastly inexperienced skier this probably wasn't a sound idea to be tackling challenging hills but they were delightfully good sports about any lacking which existed on my part. They would always wait for me to catch up, or let me go ahead and then follow. We stuck to Blue Squares and single Black Diamonds (which tested everything I had in me at the time).

When you share a lift with someone over and over again during the course of nine hours your lives tend to spill out. John was engaged to be married, the only other thing I recall 22 years later, is that he was from Cleveland, Ohio, and he was a C-level executive in the steel industry.

Après ski the guys invited me back to their condo for dinner. Yes, it might have been remarkably naïve of me to go, but I either have a slew of guardian angels protecting me or I am incredibly lucky—or both! As never, in nearly 35 years of this kind of risky behaviour, has anything remotely bad ever happen to me.

They were going to cook their steaks on the stove top—"Uh, guys you have this amazing fire in the fireplace. Can you please hand me the racks from the oven?" Dinner came out perfect. David Lynch's *Wild at Heart*© sound track in the background. Great conversation.

Three weeks later, typed on a manual typewriter in Courier font, the following poem arrived in the mail.

```
. . . Terri . . . . . . . . extraordinary!
so . . . lady shooting star surprise
with all that fire in your eyes
where is it that you want to go
what is it that you need to know?

when flying fast on powder snow
where is life, what does it show
is adrenalin rush the only role
or to soothe a hurt within a soul

the words flow easy, so much to tell
a lovely voice and you say it so well
as time goes by you must often find
people impressed by your quickness of mind

there's one thing that you do know well
that you cannot live in bland pastel
but you live and love in hues
of reds and blacks and sometimes blues
perhaps you need forever hope
the magic colours of kaleidoscope
t'is oh so warm and so appealing
To fill the time with sweet hot feeling
```

```
love is a drug, so please beware
it can sear your soul beyond repair
you can't go back once you do start
to feed the hunger in the heart

with smiles and happiness fill your days
sadness already cuts in so many ways
soar to the top and speak with the sun
frolic in life—leave nothing undone

eyes with laughter and soul with a song
the essence of living so warm and so strong
and sail away on silver moonbeams . . . .
and sail away on seas of new dreams . . . .

John
```

How can anyone begin to express the awe and wonder of receiving such from someone barely known for exactly one day? What prompts such effort from one stranger to another? I can't begin to guess. I don't recall there being a return address to thank him. Maybe the fates will conspire for that to happen now. John should know just how treasured this effort has been to me for the last 20 years.

To address all of you thinking precisely what my girlfriend Amy expressed, no, nothing remotely untoward occurred with John, not even a kiss. Her very reasonable 'why not?' (a bit more graphically expressed) can be answered equally with there was not the least bit of that illusive sexual attraction between two people that make affairs happen and even if there had been I was still legally married and I wouldn't give my husband grounds for divorce on the basis of adultery.

To accord the effort the appropriate level of respect I had the poem easel framed and matted on black, with gold ink lines framing black, blue and red handmade Italian marbled papers. Three weeks into writing **All That I Need** I picked up the poem and said a silent 'wow' to myself. Outside influences I have ignored, which echo in John's words "the words flow easy, so much to tell" seem to have made this book destined to be written since, at least, 1989?

Our histories are imprinted on us at the cellular level—literally. Our senses convey signals captured by our brains through a complex and never ending series of chemical and electronic impulses. With that in mind, think of your MOST perfect summer day. Got it in your head? Can you recall what you were wearing? Who you were with? Where you were? The specific tastes associated with that special day?

I have shared one July 4th memory already, but here are two more, noteworthy for the extremity of their similarities and differences—both involve beer and foreign men.

In the first, it's 2001 and I have been invited to join the Streits, dear German friends, for a trip home for the long weekend celebration around the 180th anniversary of Michael's fraternity. Michael, his brother, his father and grandfather before him and on, and on back to 1821, have all been members. *Mein Deutsche ist kleine Kinder deutsch* but I am 'all in' for the adventure. I force myself not to be embarrassed by my pronunciation or grammar and at least try to speak German throughout the weekend. I am the only American to be in attendance. I am not a girlfriend and certainly not a wife so the odds of my being included on any level is so astonishingly rare no one can think of any previous time this has happened. This is so cool!

I take the train from Karlsruhe. The Streits meet me at the station so I can easily find and check into the same hotel they are staying in. Gabi is very tired and pregnant and their toddler Dorothea needs a nap. I am invited by Michael to join him in spending the afternoon at his fraternity house. This IS NOTHING LIKE Animal House.© Corps Franconia is a grand stuccoed, stone and tiled roofed towered mansion built in the late 1800's complete with a huge balustraded terrace overlooking the Neckar River and Tübingen's old market square. Round One, there's not a single guy resembling James Belushi in sight. The terrace is mostly current Corps Franconia zu Tübingen fraternity members, twenty two tall, impossibly handsome, chiseled jaw, multi-lingual, hyper-intelligent charmers ranging in age from 19 to 28. Every one of them bears a scar on their person from fencing—a 'first blood' rite of passage engaged with real foils and no masks. On my friend Michael, his is near his eye—crazy machismo stuff. I am dressed in a white linen skirt and blouse, men stand as Michael introduces me, the back of my hand is kissed, courtly bows accompany and without exception each offers his seat to me. Almost immediately a tall, cold Hefeweizen with a slice of orange is brought to me. It's 80 degrees, no one knows why it's so hot and all apologise, repeatedly, as if they had control over the weather. At one point I am told my German is quite good and am asked where I learned to speak as it carries 'a charming sing-song Italian accent' (quite an accomplishment given the nature of the German language, that I am not Italian and have never been to Italy); I am pretty sure I can hear Goethe rolling over in his grave! My German is totally inadequate; every one of their English language skills is near idiomatically perfect—so much for trying to refine my German! At the next scheduled event that evening their ages will top 90, all wearing their green and pink and gold banded hat, crested jackets, and ties—it's still stiflingly hot, how do they do it? Some I meet will use their English for the first time since being Prisoners of War fifty years previous—all are equally gallant, effusive that an American is amongst them for this special occasion.

For the present, standing before me with a small silver tray bearing a second glass glistening pale gold in the afternoon sunlight is their (then) current president, 28; his astonishing presence commanding not simply because he's well over 6'4" and being incredibly man-beautiful but because of his accompanying easy confidence at his role in the world. A small speech of formal welcome, teasing acknowledgement of a pending gift to me from the fraternity in conjunction with 'your American Independence Day,' the beer is then presented with a flourish and a hand gesture commands the stereo system to life, now blasting over, and echoing across, the medieval square below us can be heard The Beach Boys! Willkommen Fraulein. Vielen Dank. By the way, beer never tasted so good.

In the second, America's consummate summer game of baseball is being shared with my friend Juan Carlos, a Cuban émigré (via Hungary and Canada) now American citizen, and his Cuban brother-in-law. We're not at any baseball game, no, we're at Fenway Park in Boston and the Red Socks© are playing the Toronto Blue Jays. You 'feel' nearly 100 years (Fenway opened in 1912) of fellow spectators squeezed, layered together in the love of the game. The cherished Green Monster™ looms. The smell of baseball lingers—

Cracker Jack,© stale beer, hot dogs, ice cream and peanuts. Dads with their kids. "Cold beer here," chanted over and over to the point that even if you don't really want one, you need one to complete your place in the montage. There is NO PLACE in America that resonates so sublimely about all that is great about this game and our country (okay, I will give Wrigley and Doubleday Fields their due) as Fenway Park on a bright blue day in July. When the Star-Spangled Banner plays my eyes fill with tears of gratitude (see Reciprocity chapter) to be in this place with a man who took enormous risk to be able to sit here today. Humbled to be born here and not have to claw my way, the long way around, to home.

The seats, far closer to the field than Kevin Costner and James Earl Jones enjoyed in *Field of Dreams*,© are along the third base line, sunshine spills over us, I can hear in my head the refrain of a pitch perfect soliloquy:

> *The one constant through all the years has been baseball. America has rolled by like an army of steamrollers. It's been erased like a blackboard, rebuilt, and erased again. But baseball has marked the time. This field, this game, is a part of our past. It reminds us of all that once was good, and what could be again.*
> —James Earl Jones, as Terrence Mann, in *Field of Dreams* (1989)

It's why we're here today. Because I wanted to share the quintessential American experience, somehow try to replicate the absolute joy I experienced at my first Red Sox game, with my Cuban friends. Because the main message of the film—'if you build it, he will come' certainly applies to the new life my friend Juan Carlos has carved out for himself.

When I moved to Boston in 1998 one of the first things I did was called the Red Sox box office for a ticket.

Only one?

Yes, it's just me.

Okay, where would you like to sit? What game?

As close to home plate as possible. It doesn't matter who the Sox are playing.

Hang on a minute.

Silence. Tick-tock.

Are you still there?'

Yes.

What's Wednesday night like for you?

I think I am going to be in Fenway Park and it's going to be perfect.

Did you find a nice ticket?

I think you'll be happy. You need to pick up your ticket at Will Call.

Wednesday comes. I take the T, Boston's subway, to Commonwealth Ave at Kenmore Square and join the masses. Collect my ticket. Smell history. Smell baseball. Participate in the joyful ritual of our nation's past time. Ushers direct. I follow. Finally, on a chill May evening I emerge from the corridor/tunnel and am guided to my seat. OMG, really? Second row. First box left of home plate, first seat on the wall.

Stars dance across the blue-black Boston sky. The moon makes her appearance. The four seats next to me fill with two dads, each with an under 10 year old son in tow. Unknown to each other before tonight they are united by a love of the game and the voracious appetites of prepubescent boys. I am astonished at what they manage to eat over the course of 9 innings. The younger, is more animated. Stands on his seat screaming, "Hit it out of the park Mo (Vaughn)" "Hit the Prudential Center Mo"; a greater state of bliss is unlikely, return on my $30 ticket price? Incalculable.

My first visit to Cooperstown© was slung with hard rain, mid-week, deserted. Stand before Ted Williams and Jackie Robinson's plaques. Watch black and white reel-to-reel film now on continuous loop video of the women's leagues, Cal Ripken's jersey, breathe *b a s e b a l l* quietly and reverently, buy a t-shirt I wish they still made.

Wonder why this sport I was never exposed to as a child became my form of rebellion and balm—there are worse things of course, but to a hockey loving father you'd never know it. Maybe it's the romance of little boys with their T-balls littering yards who dream of sliding into home plate, scoring the winning run in the bottom of the 9th. Maybe it's the odds against making it to the major leagues, the dedication required, the possibilities of injury to young muscles and bones to overcome. It could be the seeming innocence of it all, though we all, however cynical, know it's not. I recall watching my nephew Ryan as a junior in high school pitch at the state tournament. His impossibly long arms and legs winding up and then spinning like an old fashioned whirly-gig and thinking there was nothing more perfect to watch. Whatever else he accomplishes with his life, I hope he makes it to The Show!

7 water

As a child Narcissus was beautiful and he came to maturity, grew even more so. Sadly, his vanity knew no end.

By the age of sixteen he had left a trail of broken hearts from rejected lovers of both sexes. A man named Ameinias (more commonly known as Nemesis) was one of Narcissus' most ardent admirers. Narcissus responded by sending his suitor a sword, telling him to prove his adoration. Ameinias proceeded to plunge the sword into his heart, committing suicide to demonstrate his love, but not before he beseeched the gods to punish the vain Narcissus.

The goddess of the hunt, Diana, heard the plea and made Narcissus fall in love, but a fitting unrequited love. (You absolutely never want to mess around with what Diana can unleash on you!)

At Donacon in Thespia Narcissus came upon a spring and a clear pool and, for the first time, caught sight of his reflection. Over and over he tried to touch the exquisite person staring back at him from the water only to distort the image each time he reached for it. Narcissus was tormented that his beloved kept moving away from his touch. Finally unable to stand his agony further Narcissus plunged a dagger in his heart and died.

The flower is named for him and to mark his returning beauty each spring just as his reflection did after the pool calmed from his touch.

We all look at ourselves in the mirror. Unlike Narcissus I have a pretty healthy perspective on my 'overall attractiveness factor' (I think I am a solid 6 out of 10) but what's inside my head and my heart have ALWAYS, and in all ways, been so much more important to me and my well-being. Frankly, I think it's a perfect waste of that clear, beautiful water simply being a mirror to reflect our images.

Narcissus pined. I swim.

Ever watch a baby in her bath water splash and giggle and enjoy her yellow rubber duck or her frog sponge? The neighborhood kids run through the sprinkler or slide on their bellies on those Waveriders©? When did you lose that particular level of enjoyment about bath time? Or swimming? Or wading in a creek stream, the tactile pleasure of smooth stones or the unique mud of the bed squishing up between your toes? When was the last time you stood in the rain for the pure delight which can be derived from being caught in the skies opening up, rather than cursing your misfortune of leaving the umbrella at home and the water spots now on your suit?

We spend nine months floating around in the amniotic fluid of our mother's wombs. Our bodies contain between 90 and 94% water. If Darwin and the evolutionists are to be believed, 'long ago' our ancestors climbed up out of the water onto land and began the metamorphosis into ape and eventually man. As such, it makes sense that the place we would feel most comfortable is in water but a great many of us are scared to death we are going to drown. I listened to an example of this coming from a 7-year-old boy who had worked himself up into such a state about being in the swimming pool taking lessons that he might have drown were it not for the patience and composure of his instructor. Equally so, but without the theatrics, a professional athlete in nearly perfect physical form struggling with his breathing and buoyancy to the degree he later confessed he thought the lifeguards were going to have to drag his 6' 5" frame out of the pool.

Here's a tip to rational adults to overcome that fear; flip over on your back, relax, put your arms out level with your shoulders and tip your head a little back and look up at the sky—breathe. SEE? You float. Nothing scary happens. Why? Two reasons. First we are actually 'less dense' than the water (it applies to fresh, salt and chlorinated). I actually issue a prayer to God in this attitude each morning as I finish up my swim. Second, as the rest of our body follows our spine. When you tip your head back to look at the sky your legs, arms and torso assume the most comfortable natural position—as long as you relax the water will hold you.

Some of you are thinking, 'ugh, no way am I going to be caught dead in a bathing suit in front of people.' Get over yourself. I can absolutely assure you that unless you are a man over a certain age trying to squeeze yourself into a Speedo© bikini four sizes too small no one is going to pay the least attention to you. Honest, it is astonishing how all those gallons of water serve as camouflage once you are submerged!

We're in the water to feel good, or feel better. We're there in that big blue lagoon, cove, swimming hole in a river or lap pool to enjoy the cool water caressing our bodies. Some of us are there to get stronger and leaner and fitter doing untold numbers of laps of freestyle, back and breast stroke and desperately trying to synch up our arms and legs to comply with the demands of the butterfly stroke. We're there with our kick boards, fins and hand paddles and stop watches because getting back in the water gives us a time of absolute quiet where we can push ourselves physically without the danger of getting hurt. And where, at least for myself who ceased be a serious athlete when I left high school, I managed to shave more than 7 1/2 inches off my waist (not to mention everywhere else) in a mere three months.

I have lived near the ocean frequently enough to absolutely ache with longing when I don't. The first technology company I worked for was based in Elmsford, NY, but I figured out it was only a 20 minute commute from Old Greenwich, CT so I could live near the ocean. I rented a converted carriage house with a covered porch the width of the building on Binney Lane, the Binney family founded Crayola Crayons,© my front door being less than 40 feet from high water mark of the cove. My front yard, part of Long Island Sound, had a swim platform about 3/4 of a mile out; I would swim to it as swell, tides and wave height permitted from May to September's end.

When I moved to Boston, Massachusetts for subsequent roles at other technology firms the rocky shores of Rockport and Marblehead of Boston's North Shore were like polar lodestones to me. The wide swath of sand spanning Swampscott and Lynn's waterfront became my front yard in a move to the suburbs. A couple of times a year (off season) I still drive to Rockport and check into The Linden Tree Inn. Pre-dawn I walk down to the Front Street Beach and plunge into the bracing North Atlantic, high tide is best as it's further out to the swim platform and really cold. The town is still sleeping and I am absolutely alone in the water. I cannot touch bottom by treading water or even diving. On some level as I flip and drive myself beneath the surface I am a mermaid (I really do try to keep my ankles together as a giant tail fin and not kick them separately) scanning the bottom for bits of old crockery, sea glass and sea shells (I assure you I am benign in my siren call and would never think of wrecking sailing vessels on the rocks). And then I begin my work-out swimming the width of the harbour, repeatedly just near the platform. There's always a sea gull sitting there (if not a cormorant) tipping its head back and forth at me I am sure wondering if with all my under the water disappearing why I am not bringing up a fish! At those times of year and certainly the time of day, I am so far out I couldn't be saved if something did happen (there's a bit of adrenaline rush to be found in that by the way) back and forth for an hour or so (there's a clock on the Opera House tower clearly visible). I swim until the sun rises and starts reflecting off the windows into my eyes and people are on the beach bundled in their sweaters, coffee cups in hand, dogs off leash fetching sticks or balls thrown into the surf. At which point it's time to come in, scoop up my sea treasures and go have some breakfast.

There's something absolutely sublime about being in the waters of Traigh Bhan (Gaelic for White Strand) which fronts my friend John McLean's bit of the Isle of Iona called Lagandorain (Gaelic for place of the otters). Iona is where St. Columba first brought Christianity to Scotland in the 6th Century, the monastery is walking distance to John's home; these waters are a very special kind of baptism to be sure. I have been blessed to swim here twice—turning an interesting shade of blue from the cold, nothing to be traded for the experience. Striking are the looks of natives and pilgrims alike walking atop the sand dune overlooking these waters in parka's and hats and mittens and me, sans wet suit, serving as the 'attraction of the day.' If you aren't a 'water baby' this type of behaviour is likely very hard to comprehend.

Maybe I am so drawn to the cleansing, therapeutic nature of being in water because as an Aquarian (an astrological air sign) I am seen pouring my amphorae of water out, quenching the thirst of the heavens and all its inhabitants below. Maybe I immerse myself in cool blue lagoons to fill back up so I can give away more sustenance away. As my 'Diana' friend Jenn maintains there is one word I should learn and embrace as my mantra and it is discernment—she's keen to point out that not everyone I meet is worthy of my energy, time and most specifically my loving kindness. If you remember the Love Is . . . cartoons, "Love isn't love until you give it away" kind of stuck with me but it has been a draining burden at times to be so free with my energy.

When I started swimming (again) it was because I intellectually couldn't handle the idea of being the fat girl on my bike out on the road (adults can be just as cruel as kids). The distorted privacy accorded by millions of gallons of water is a balm to those of us struggling with fitness. Swimming, it seemed to me, was the perfect way to get some exercise in and not hurt myself in the process (thus setting myself back and not doing anything again until healing could take place). As it's generally regarded as the best possible overall workout to tone while building endurance—why would anyone not swim?

I am not going to lie to you dear reader and say I am or was comfortable admitting that I needed a size 18 or putting such a size in a turquoise Speedo on my body. The truth is I hated it. What prompted this was measuring the waists of my skinniest clothes — beautiful, and expensive, things from the 1980's and discovering that my waist was now (shocking) nearly 19 inches larger! WHAT?!! How/when did I get SO OUT OF SHAPE?

I started with 20 minutes four times a week in May. By June, when I joined an Intermediate Adult Group Swim group lesson, I was doing an hour of backstroke and breast stroke with leg drills EACH DAY but I was now wearing an obnoxious orange Speedo in a 16 (still not a good look but both suits had been dirt cheap). At the end of July I was able to fit into (not beautifully) a lemon yellow size 12. BUT, the real sense of accomplishment for me wasn't my shrinking physique, though it is certainly really nice that I am being successful at reclaiming my body. No, what has happened in the midst of being in the water for 14-plus hours a week is I got (relatively speaking) crazy fast!

Six sessions in our teacher, and the club aquatics director, got out the stopwatch. Three middle aged women, facing a fit late twenty-something man and a stopwatch —you are likely cringing just thinking about it, aren't you? Not one of us could do those fancy flip turns you see the likes of Dana Torres and Michael Phelps do with such ease. Tim (our 'coach') wanted us to eventually have times for swimming 50, then 200, then 500 in freestyle stroke. I swear we almost mutinied! For my own first attempt at a 'short course 50' I stopped at the far wall, gasped for repeated breathes, gulped water, issued an, "OH GOD" and heard Tim yell the length of the pool, "SWIM!" I came in at 1:03 and some change. (Actually, considering where I started, 'not bad.') I had already been swimming for more than an hour before this, Patricia and Tulin are not morning people and so the three of us agreed 200 metres 'for time' was not going to be possible. To our credit we stayed in the water and swam the 200 metres without out the watch. We couldn't dodge the bullet the next week. I had worked on my 50 during the week but the 200 stymied me. My time shrank down to 54 seconds, the next week 51 seconds, and then astonishingly 50 seconds all still without a flip turn. To express my shock and delight on paper wouldn't begin to share with you the total scene at the shallow end of the pool.

Tim and three lifeguards on duty congratulated me on my stroke, my speed, and encouraged me to nail my flip turn so I could shave more time off and, then, they actually applauded me. I am emotional normally. All the little progresses you've made over three months' time have amounted to doing something you never imagined doing, having really competent swimmers notice, encourage you and cheer you on and then you get to honour them and yourself in swimming 50 metres in less than 26 seconds off the current women's World Record (23.73 Britta Steffen of Germany who happens to be 22 years my junior) is overwhelming. You bet I cried; the most deliriously happy, sobbing grateful tears. I asked if I got a silver star and as we have a club meet coming up for the kids Tim said a medal wasn't a problem and how proud he was of me.

Then he was back to being my taskmaster; okay let's get your 200 with splits (split times are how fast you swim each 50 yards or metres of the 200). Oh, come on Tim you are kidding me right? Nope, ready when you are, in three, two, one. Funny how he knew I could do this even if I didn't!

The week before my 200 yards was a disaster. I was only able to swim 100 of it as freestyle before stopping and given 'a get out of jail free card' to continue swimming the second 100 in breast stroke (easier to be sure but so much slower than a properly executed freestyle stroke). My time for this funky mixed 200 was 5:13. Suffice to say I was so not looking forward to coming off my 50 yard high and tackling this again.

Off I go. Flutter kick, kick, kick, stroke and breathe (repeat). Wall, turn, kick, kick, kick, stroke and breathe (repeat), eight lengths, seven turns. Last length feeling like I am gulping water and… Not. Going. To. Make. It. Just ahead on the bottom of the pool through my goggles, I see the tiled T lane marking, almost there… in my head. KICK. DAMN IT. KICK. JUST. TOUCH. THE. FUCKING. WALL. OhMyGaawd! Pant, pant, pant, fling goggles off.

Well? Well?

Tim has this HUGE grin on his face, shaking his head slightly. Not only did I swim the whole thing continuously in freestyle (an almost impossible to comprehend improvement in endurance in a single weeks' time) but I have shaved nearly 45 seconds off my 200 yards. WHAT?? FORTY-FIVE SECONDS? The lifeguards' jaws drop and then, smiles and all nod approval. Better still when he shares my split times with me each 50 is within sight of the others by no more than 11 seconds. Now, I really cry. I have learned to pace myself. SO COOL.

I can't get over that something which was not EVER been on my bucket list has not just astonished me but those people who have seen me in the pool every morning, two hours a day, for three months making baby step improvements to THIS. NOW. WOW!

Immediately following the "time trials" and feeding off all the encouragement accorded me to nail my flip turn, I practiced 20 flip turns in a row. The next day 40, skipped a day and then back at it with another 60 and now, where my confidence was seriously lacking (and fear of whacking my head, heels, ankles, toes) I can honestly say that I do my flip turn with the enthusiasm of a six-year-old having the training wheels off her bicycle. This is the stuff of magic and it's inside each and every one of us just waiting to be tapped, refined, encouraged, polished and celebrated.

The very coolest aspect of all this is the 'without trying' factor. To quote the Reverend Robert H. Schuller, "What great thing would you attempt if you knew you could not fail?"

Tim Auerhahn, for believing, encouraging, pushing, and hiring an amazing, talented crew who did the same for me when you weren't around . . . THANK YOU!

8 reciprocity

When he was 13, Philip II King of Macedonia hired the Greek philosopher Aristotle to be his son Alexander's (The Great) personal tutor (can you imagine learning from Aristotle? How cool would that be?). In 340BC, as Philip invaded Thrace, he left his then 16 years old son as regent with the power to rule Macedonia in his absence. As we know from history, by the time Alexander was 22 he was king in his own right, by 30 he had created one of the largest empires of the ancient world. He was dead, poisoned, at the age of 33.

Elizabeth I ascended the English throne in 1558 at 25 years of age. She inherited an impoverished country torn apart by religious intolerance. She ruled successfully for 45 years because her approach to politics was cautious, conservative and serious. The England she left behind at her death on the 24th of March 1603 was one of the most powerful and prosperous countries in the world.

In no way does my youth, or frankly that of 99% the teenagers and twenty-somethings on the planet, come close to the capabilities and achievements of these two historic wunderkinds. And yet, when I was 17 I became the youngest licensed tour guide in Niagara Falls (on either side of the border) which my employer had ever hired. Out of the exhaustive exams requiring proficiency in geology, history, quirky facts, Native American culture, fundamentals of hydro-electricity and dare-devil attempts I had the second highest scores for all three years I had this job—one that not only did I love, but excelled at. I was 'good enough' that my average hourly rate with tips was about $25 in 1979, 1980 and 1981. In my first season I found it incredible that I was teaching 40 year high school history teachers 'how to be' tour guides. I discovered in myself the natural ability/gift of taking HUGE bodies of information, condensing it down to the most salient points and making it relevant to my audience. This job was the reason I changed my major from Interior Design to Journalism, Broadcast and Speech and then more specifically Communications.

It's never been lost on me the enormous responsibility which I was entrusted at such a tender age including driving a large white minivan carrying 14 people from every corner of the planet. My job was to provide information and amusement, cross international borders and navigate passport controls, adhere to time schedules, walk upwards of 7 miles a day in 3" white high heels, a long sleeved blouse with a big floppy bow and a wrap-around skirt. I always carried a huge multi-coloured umbrella open not only to keep myself in the sight of my charges in a sea of humanity but to stay out of the sun. Being a tour guide helped to define me; in truth, every job I have held subsequently has embraced elements of this special first one. There are a million stories when you have a job like this, like almost being fired because I refused to leave North Koreans at the Canadian Border alone and didn't get the van back in time for the next tour shift. I digress.

I believe with my whole being that the greatest chance any of us have for remaining relevant as we age is to have friendships which span every decade of the human lifespan. Mentor youthful friends with your experiences; the positive and the things you have screwed up royally. Ensure that you stay in a place of alert observation by opening your mind to the possibilities that lay acutely before your young friends but are no less relevant because you own decades.

The gift of knowledge, the time committed to convey that knowledge, the reciprocity of getting it, applying it and succeeding pays honour to both teacher and student. Far too many people limit their growth by imposing some ridiculous chronologically acceptable age parameter around from whom they will learn. In 1975 my English teacher Mr Takahara actually requested a copy of a poem I had written (I was 14) about the ending of the Vietnam War, to keep, for his own pleasure. We're N-E-V-E-R too old, or too young, to teach or to learn.

The beautiful thing about approaching everything in life with enthusiasm is that other people respond and it magnifies and multiplies the experience. The contagion happens because when you challenge yourself and accomplish a tiny goal others around you (who care) will set the bar a little higher for you knowing full well you will try and maybe even surpass expectations; our own and theirs.

In the summer of 2011 I acquired a self-appointed swim coach and friend Owen Drinkwater (33 years my junior, wise beyond his years, truly an amazing teacher and a whole cheer-leading section in his own right). He got it in his head that I should try 'head to head' drills. I will explain because as a non-competitive swimmer I hadn't a clue what he was talking about and most of you reading this certainly couldn't be expected to.

At each end of a competition pool there is something called a flagpole. It's not really a pole with a flag on it so much as a taunt rope run between two poles mounted on either side of the width of the pool which helps swimmers recognise they are approaching the wall or the end of their race. If you ever watch swim races this is also often the point of the last breath a swimmer will take before reaching the wall—regardless of whether it's the end of the race or there's more swimming to be done. Let me assure you that without lots of practice this is nearly impossible to get enough air into your lungs, not take another breath while swimming as fast as you possibly can, get to the wall, flip (still don't breathe), shimmer, rise to the surface, and take a breath on your SECOND stroke. I have a new found respect for anyone that can do this and make it seem 'normal'—it's ridiculously HARD!

In a head-to-head drill you sprint swim from just on the backside of the flag pole to the wall, execute a flip turn, and then swim back to the other side of the flag pole. A perfect swimmer will actually push off the wall with such force that they emerge from the water the first time someplace on the other side of the flag pole. From the time your head passes the flag pole on the way in, to the point it passes on the way out is timed. According to Owen, VERY FAST high school boys swim this sprint in about 4 seconds. I want to put into perspective that such swimmers as Owen referenced have been swimming competitively since they were 5, with tens of thousands of hours in the pool and very likely a couple hundred thousand flip turns under their Speedo's. On the other hand—there's me; an overweight and 50 and ½-year-old female with absolutely no previous competitive swimming experience or desire to swim for speed.

While intellectually I understood what a freestyle stroke was, until less than three months before this occasion, I certainly had never swum a single stroke of it. Until four weeks previously I could barely swim 50 yards of freestyle stroke continuously and until three weeks prior to this 'flag pole drill' adventure I had never attempted a flip turn.

The previous day I took my weekly 'intermediate adult swim lesson' with one of Owen's lifeguard colleagues Doug Leclair (18, also a competitive swimmer, also about to go off to study pre-med). For the better part of the hour Doug brilliantly split himself between myself and his other pupil each swimming at different degrees of competency in two lanes. We worked on improving my stroke (for speed) and tweaking my flip turn from my former gymnast adaptation of thrust forward, hard tuck, rotate 180 degrees, instead of the muscle memory which dictated I rotate 360 degrees, plant feet on the wall at 12 o'clock and push hard off the wall to a dip-your-chin-flop-your-legs (your feet follow your head), push off the wall swimmer flip turn.

The mere idea of doing a speed drill attempting to combine a perfectly executed flip turn and my 'less than 24 hours old' still developing new (faster and more aggressive tweaked) freestyle stroke mentally made me want to puke in the pool. BUT! Owen's belief in my ability, his encouragement, his gift of time (okay, and no one else was in the pool) plus his knowledge as a competitive swimmer in tandem with my own desire to keep refining my form and function in the water spurred me on.

Owen: "Come on Terri, it'll be fun." And he explains where he'll start and stop timing me, and what I have to do. In fairness 'fun' is not the word which came to mind.

Me: "You are one sick dude. Fine. I'll try."

Owen: "Ready when you are."

Me: Mental growl. Goggles back in place, back up past the flag pole line another 4 feet or so to actually have a starting point of momentum before I cross the flag-pole. Off I go for my initial attempt.

Owen: "8 seconds" (possibly a couple tenths and a couple hundredths of a second in addition).

Me: "I am not leaving this pool today until I get to 6.5"

Owen, and Sue (the other lifeguard on duty): "Terri you are talking about shaving 1.5 seconds off your time, on something you've never done before, in a single day!"

Me: "Yes, and this makes hour number 3 since I started swimming this morning but I am not quitting today until I accomplish this." At this point, hungry, very tired, more than a bit sore, and definitely approaching prune state on feet and hands their very reasonable doubts mirror my physical state. I should mention that the following times are conveyed with Owen's perfect recall—evidently he once (for fun) memorized a string of Pi numbers two hundred and thirty some odd characters long.

My next drill time comes in at 7.9 seconds. Then 7.49, and in successive attempts 7.29, 7.09, 7.00, and then, I have no idea where this came from, I manage the drill in 6.48 in less than 15 minutes. Yay-baby! The look on both Owen and Sue's faces are a state of exuberant joy co-mingled with jaw-dropping disbelief. While I wanted to perform this consistently at 6.5 or under, my next 10 efforts were around 6.7 or 6.8 seconds unless I totally missed my foot placement on the wall and then I was back up at 7.1. Only one more was under my 6.5-second threshold and the last one I attempted for the day came in at 6.57 seconds—I made my goal. I am humbled. I am blessed. I receive the gift of Owen's encouragement and honour him and his years in the pool with doing something I didn't know I wanted (or needed) to do. And then, I cry, again. And then I very gratefully got out of the pool.

A half an hour's worth of work and suddenly I find that I am just 2.5 seconds off the time which 'really fast high school boys' do this drill. TWO AND ONE HALF SECONDS! Sue later tells me that Owen shared that it takes him a year or more to take two seconds off his time in any drill, making my achievement over a period of 30 minutes all that more incomprehensible—to all three of us.

Owen had another gift for me an hour later as I headed back out to the pool after I de-chlorinated and dressed to thank him. He said that he and Sue had just been talking about me and how my dedication was inspiring for both of them. As Sue moved to another lifeguard stand for her rotation, Owen then further startled me by candidly admitting that dealing with tears of gratitude was something new to him and he didn't know how to respond. He wasn't put off, or scared or intimidated or thought it weird, he didn't feel the need to escape; this man/boy of 17 put squarely at my feet his desire to understand gratitude tears. Note to Owen's parents, congratulate yourselves, you have raised a truly extraordinary young man.

One of my less endearing nicknames in high school was Weeping Willow. I couldn't tell you why I was reminded of this chapter of my life with these particular tears. Obviously, in terms of peer pressure, it wasn't always easy being so in touch with my emotions. What was then meant as a cutting remark I have come to embrace as the highest compliment.

Every male of my acquaintance, and likely yours, has a very difficult time coping with the tears of another adult, especially a female adult. Angry, sad, hurt, disappointed tears are hard enough. The (seeming) vulnerability, the inability to 'fix' what's wrong all seem to emasculate a man who is our friend, lover, partner. Guys, first and foremost please understand that tears are a wonderful way of purging toxins from our endocrine system. The logic behind this will be lost in the moment as you read this but try to stash this away for future reference. I can't explain exactly what happens to us from a medical standpoint but please believe me there is nothing healthier than a good, purging cry.

This brings me to the crying that all of my friends over the years and most recently my new lifeguard friends and swim instructors (Owen, Doug, Mollie, Tim, Michele, Kyle, Chelsea, Sue, Anna among them) have witnessed throughout the summer of 2011; one that I am utterly capable of issuing without societal or cultural constraints on a regular basis; tears of gratitude.

Gratitude tears are vastly different from 'normal' tears. For me they always begin with a tiny burst of 'white light' in my solar plexus region. They are at once visceral and, I believe, Divine in origin. There is always a constriction in my throat concurrent with my heart feeling as if it will burst not from pain but from love. I make an effort to simultaneously collect myself and put what I have just experienced and my feelings about it into perspective so that I can relive the whole as a cherished memory in the future. These tears are certainly emotional but in a 'perfection' way that is hard to explain. Gosh, if you have to cry isn't this far more preferable than as a result of sadness? These tears flow not in sobs but spill over the edge of my lower eyelids much like the overflow of a mill pond over its race sluice. These are physical evidence of the power of living in gratitude, fully and completely present in every moment.

If these tears occur in a sacred place such as a church sanctuary I refer to them as 'getting the passions.' My namesake Saint Teresa of Avila is the patron saint of people in need of grace. She wrote a seminal piece of Spanish Renaissance literature called *El Camino de Perfección* (The Way of Perfection). If you are an art historian or a more pedestrian fan of *The da Vinci Code*, Bernini's *The Ecstasy of St. Teresa* opens wide doors of interpretation of the true nature of Teresa's ecstasy. I never knew, until I started writing this particular chapter, that Teresa frequently experienced what she described as a rich 'blessing of tears.' As you might imagine, I was blown away at the synchronicity of our reaction to the gift of tears.

Even having years of experience with them, how do you begin to explain something like tears of gratitude to anyone who has yet to feel such grace? In this particular instance someone whose life years are less than two-score and is about to head off to study pre-med and then medicine because he's 'always wanted to help people.' Someone who, if he can maintain the beauty which exists within him at this moment, I believe will accomplish amazing things and impact mankind in unimaginable ways.

Owen, only you can know if I came close to making sense of gratitude tears from an intellectual perspective for you. Most importantly to understand them completely only comes from living each moment of your life in humility for the tiny, yet often significant, gifts that define us and our lives.

9 wisdom from the swamp

Size matters not. Look at me. Judge me by my size, do you? Hmm? Hmm. And well you should not. For my ally is the Force, and a powerful ally it is. Life creates it, makes it grow. Its energy surrounds us and binds us. Luminous beings are we, not this crude matter. You must feel the Force around you; here, between you, me, the tree, the rock, everywhere, yes. Even between the land and the ship.
—Stars Wars,© George Lucas and Lucasfilm, Ltd.

I am sufficiently self-effacing to realise that I have a finite amount of patience and a natural inclination to avoid raising my voice. As a result, I believe I would have either been a terrible mom or a health wreck from the related stress of trying too hard to contain my frustration. Being a mom has to be the most difficult job on the planet to do really, really, well. So I embraced the next best thing. I love being an aunt, and I am very good at it. The 'sugar-them-up-and-give-them-back' aspect has worked out perfectly over the course of the last thirty years of my life. Initially baking cookies with them and teaching them to respect the water and how to dive safely, taking them to pick strawberries (not recommended for little girls who hate dirt and bugs), sometimes teaching them to drive and eventually taking them on their first (not-with-the parents) overnight road-trip to see Dave Matthews Band in concert 5 hours one-way away.

Notwithstanding my perception of my maternal abilities I love kids for a hundred million reasons, not the least of which is every single day is the greatest adventure for them to experience. They respond to kindness in equal measure with devotion and affection. They love unconditionally, and especially when we, as adults, give them the opportunity to build their confidence and gently challenge them to do more and encourage their natural gifts.

I have mentioned my swim instructor Doug Leclair previously. When he took over our group lesson after 8 weeks of instruction from his boss Tim he put Christina and I through a let's-see-what-ya-got session. Doug sat on the bottom of the pool cross-legged in five and a half feet of water for an extraordinary length of time watching every detail. Then he started tweaking everything that wasn't quite right.

What he's done to help my developing swim strokes is humbly accepted but the responsibility is mine alone to apply his instruction. I discovered that because I have been flutter-kicking with bent knees (splashing is BAAADDD!), instead of focusing on the use of my hip flexors and kicking with my whole leg, I have been swimming my freestyle stroke all wrong!!! Just this little tweak has me totally winded once again after swimming a 50. Evidently using your legs properly requires MORE OXYGEN, who knew? I take solace that this burn in my quadriceps is torquing the remaining cellulite on my thighs! What else am I not remembering correctly? Why can't I get this variation on the flip turn by myself the way that I seem to be able to when Doug is watching? Thankfully, I finally found the illusive, slight rolling action to my left on my right stroke which forms a pocket allowing me to actually take a quality breathe; consistency and eventually perfection are a long way off but I have something to build upon. Post Tim-era instruction, despite the addition of a flip turn and improved stroke, I unhappily find myself on a time plateau of 50/51 seconds for my 50 which would not budge. What is the missing connection between my mental preparation and the kinetic force I need to apply to my swim workout? "Oh yes, gee, that helps a lot Doug, use the kick board as an easel to hold the stupid (growl) stop-watch so I HAVE TO do my 50's against the clock!!!" OHGAWD, do I have to? Actually, yes I do, as it will help me honour my commitment to achieve a 43-second 50 by Thanksgiving (I hope).

In the meantime our last session together before he leaves for Fairfield University nets an unexpected breakthrough against that goal. It seems silly to be so nervous about a stop-watch that I would let it interrupt my usual blissful sleeping patterns the night before—I was COMPLETELY WIRED! And in recognizing this as my clock read 1:18AM I was certain my efforts and attention span within my lesson the next morning would be as non-existent as a 14-year-old on the last day of school.

The pre-game psyching-up sports psychologists and coaches' reference was no less real to me as a 12-week-in adult swimmer. I cannot tell you how much I personally wanted to do well, to break that 50 in 50 threshold. Equally, though ridiculous, I really didn't want Doug to feel like he had wasted four hours of his time during the month of August. The only way I felt I could ensure this was to show him that I had honoured the knowledge he had attempted to pass onto me.

I had been in the water about an hour and a half. My initial 25 yards is too fast, I am out of breath at the wall and because of that I can't get enough out of my flip turn and to push off the wall to know that I will not complete this 50 in under 50. My personal awareness of my body is shifting, certainly not 12 weeks ago and I doubt even 5 weeks previously would I have known this. I can 'feel' that I haven't paced myself properly, I bailed. My sense of my timing is spot-on. My split time is 21 seconds (which clearly means that 43 seconds is entirely doable within the three months remaining until Thanksgiving). I know that to have enough for the wall and flip turn my split time needs to be at between 23/24 seconds. We analyze and tweak, come back to the timed 50 a half an hour later.

You that feeling when you are game-on? You can't explain it, but you know it in your gut. It doesn't matter if you are giving a presentation, writing your dissertation, performing an aria or open heart surgery, or making a fabulous meal for 20 friends. There really are sublime moments when our intellect, muscle memory, training and 'the planets align.' Where something clicks and no matter how tired we might be desire and adrenalin cover the difference, we function fully aware and are wildly successful. My next timed 50 comes in at 49.9 seconds. .6 or 1.1 seconds off swimming a 50 is nothing in the scheme of the universe. Even less when you consider how many people die of abuse, starvation and war in that same time. But, in that moment, screaming Yes! Yes! YEESSSS! Slapping and splashing water like a four year old, Keegan and Doug smiling at both my achievement and my subsequent behaviour (the latter perhaps as though I have lost my mind) nothing else matters. There's no video replay, I can only hold it in my heart and head till I overflow with gratitude and the adrenalin drains from my body—where tears of gratitude will run rampant for a full ten minutes at the end of two hours of instruction and nearly three hours in the water that day. In a mere 4 weeks I have shaved more than 32 seconds off swimming my 50, the last 7 seconds may well kill me. Still I soar in ways that can't adequately be expressed; it's just 1.1 second but it seemed a miracle.

After my morning swim, every morning for nearly three months, I found myself at the edge of an energy force of goodness, patience, creativity, and unconditional love. I couldn't quite wrap my head around why in watching Doug and Owen give group lessons to little kids for a couple hours back-to-back each morning I should feel so emotionally vulnerable. I tried repeatedly to put my reaction into perspective. I knew I was in the presence of something amazing, greatness on a precipice of manifestation. Just as the summer was wrapping up, last lessons being given, readiness made for beginning his pre-med studies, I finally realised that Doug's greatest gift as an instructor has nothing to do with his remarkable ability to take adult 'students' to the next level of efficiency, and nearly kill every muscle in your body in the process, but everything to do with this 18 year old man being the swimming equivalent of Yoda (from Star Wars).

Those of you 'of a certain age' will recall Yoda was the ancient, much revered, and greatest of all Jedi Masters. Yoda lived in a swamp (okay, the blue lagoon formed by a health club pool is a bit upscale compared to Yoda's environment—and Doug physically resembles not Yoda one bit but a young John F. Kennedy, Jr.—but please stay with me here). Yoda was 900 years old and for 800 years he had trained Jedi warriors. His wisdom was vast. Yoda was ever pulling from the common surroundings to teach universal lessons of capability, overcoming fear, tapping into a Jedi warrior's own energy to overcome with, "Do, or do not. There is no 'try.'"

Each morning he'd take the three to six-year-olds on a great adventure. One day they'd be learning to trust the distance from the edge of the pool to the water and learning to jump in and 'know' that they would be safe. But it wasn't as simple as that—no, they were jumping off an intergalactic planet and coming back to Earth to rescue humankind from an alien invasion. Another day, they'd be racing across the desert (in this case the width of the kiddie pool) avoiding the float-y noodles which were rattlesnakes, to the safety of an oasis on the other side where Doug and Owen stood. Every aspect of learning to swim became a life lesson in adventure and 'the force' that was always with these kids.

Every truly great teacher has this gift. To challenge without intimidating, encourage, praise and revise lessons to resonate with the individual student and generate a passion for learning and growth. One of my own, and also for Miles and his sister Charlotte, was Jedi Master Doug bringing out 'the force' within us in the pool.

10 the girl with the mermaid tattoo

The world tends to unfold its largest to us at precisely the moment we are most able to receive its gifts. Like waiting for Christmas our lives go along predictably day-after-day and then BAMM, suddenly unexpected delights rain down upon us.

My swim instructor Tim had finished his tutorials in July to be ready to assist his wife in having their first child passed the baton of my instruction onto Doug in August, my friend Owen adding his own self-appointed and critical role in my training simultaneously, I admit their departures for university caused me an immoderate concern when suddenly, Mia Bink, certified personal trainer, entered my life.

I feebly attempted to describe Mia to my girlfriend Jenn via text messages as she was en route to guest speak at an American Express executive event in NYC.

Me: "Jenn, imagine me 25 years ago and as a personal trainer."

Jenn: "You would be gagged, duck taped, and stuffed in a closet for my safety."

When texting Mia about how I should outfit myself for our first session, she replied simply: "Bathing suit?"

Me: "Okay! That's easy. Are you suggesting Zumba© with the ancient hens? Or do you have other tortures in mind?"

Mia: "Swim from 7:30–8. short sweet love and abuse. Start keeping a food journal."

Me: "LMAO and actually I just snorted in the locker room!"

Mia: "Hahaha!!"

She is the kind of force of nature that either evokes rabid jealousy or a blend of curiosity and adoration. An example of which could be witnessed in the faces of 9 year-old boys who have no idea why they are suddenly interested in taking Aqua-Zumba© with their moms and grandmothers. She is physically presented in a twenty-something package complete with strong, healthy, voluptuously-curvy attributes including an enviable hour glass waist. A little less than half her back is adorned with a tattoo featuring a bit of the swirling ocean and a mermaid and covering half her rock hard abs is a whimsical fish. If she lived 200 years ago she would have courtesan belly dancer in silk veils and gold coins unwittingly used (or in collusion) to ensnare visiting diplomats to spill their state secrets before their formal audiences with a pasha! She suggested that her theme song, as relates to my writing this chapter, should be CocoRilie's Smokey Taboo.[©]

Mia has a high voltage, infectious laugh and a genuine concern for the physical safety of her clients—only once, 7 years previous, have I encountered such with my former trainer Ben Barrett. I am rightfully terrified of her version of "what's next" but she's aware of the goals, my physical limitations as defined by both right and left torn Achilles tendon injuries from 8 years previous and a never repaired left ACL and, as I am trading my professional marketing communications writing skills for her knowledge we're a team eager to help the other reach success. And so it begins.

There is something utterly resonant about connecting with another mermaid! Let alone one half your age who embraces the swimming elegance of Ester Williams (most of you will have to do a Wiki search) and the fantastical capabilities of Ariel, The Little Mermaid[©] both of whom were lucky enough to have gay men handling their wardrobes with liberal applications of pearls and sequins.

My swimming goals are not just about achieving a heightened proficiency in speed or about whittling my body into submission. Yes, those are seriously important but more so, as a former (a long, long time ago) gymnast I want the satisfaction of knowing that as I cut through the water achieving my goal of 43 seconds for 50 yards that my stroke and kick and every tiny detail of my swimming is beautiful in its form. I want my swimming to the equivalent of calligraphy put to vellum, the exquisite skill which in any language stands out from even the most elaborate computer type-font. I want my body to sweep nearly along on top of the water, cutting a clean path devoid of any splashing or thrashing, my flip turns perfectly executed, my breath poetically moderated.

The universe hates a vacuum and it has clearly filled my coaching void with skills equal to those of Owen, Doug and Tim. For Mia it's about 'playing with me.' She, as a competitive swimmer and someone who has taught swimming for over 9 years, assesses in short order what I am capable of and will ensure that I am challenged to be better and stronger every time we get together at the results of her coaching. I better understand how sports psychology can help an individual be more successful at life. With Mia I have someone whose own hedonism and appreciation for beauty will take my training toward a more elegant and feminine end result.

For the record, as Mia inherits my eager self, my waist hovered around 38.5 inches. I am down a total of 8.75 inches since April and want to be at 31 and hopefully at 29 by November's end. She wants a food journal—everything I eat, when I eat it, documentation put in her hands for our next session in 5 days' time. Mind you I am so NOT about deprivation. In the previous two days to this conversation I whacked out on chocolate ice cream with both caramel and marshmallow swirls and salted almonds. I don't believe cravings should be denied and I caved into them, as a result of my indulgence I am forced to swim more! Gee, what a terrible hardship to bear!

Mia says, 'show me what you've got,' this seems to be cyclical with my swim coaches. Doug and Owen had already started stripping down the elements of my kick and stroke, now it undergoes a radical smack-down! Off I go on another baseline swim 50 yards of freestyle—just how many miles have I swum this summer? In October Anna and Mia speculate it's at least the 103 miles of Diana Nyad's Cuba to Florida attempt several times over.

Mia wants me to swim with 'deliberation' and slow down, and for each 25 yards count how many strokes I take.

Hmm. I don't really multi-task well in the pool just remembering to breathe, kick with my whole leg and not from my knees, stay flat, rotate to breath, do Doug's little treble clef thingy, and, now, COUNT?!

I can't.

She does. It's 32. Evidently, not good.

Okay, do it again. Stretch out and hold the stroke until it's almost painful. Count again. GO!

23 strokes. Better.

Okay, again. The stroke should be sooooo exaggerated as to be awkward. Go!

19 strokes.

Really? Are you kidding?

Less than 10 minutes. So, why? I want to know.

Proper technique ensures muscular-skeletal integrity . . . that is to say it keeps the athlete injury free and most importantly promotes efficiency thus increasing sport performance. Each stroke a swimmer takes utilizes a unit of energy—therefore if each stroke is proficient an athlete uses less energy to travel the same distance than were improper form utilized. This conserved energy can then be used to increase speed, distance or both. Make sense?!?

Next time we get together Mia pulls out the stop-watch. Sigh. By that sigh I am not rebelling, I know that it is good for me but I would have appreciated the window of prep that allows a good psyching myself up to occur. Whipping the watch out when I am not mentally ready makes me feel like I am not going to do 'as well.'

Her newest drill is for anti-speed. Huh?

I want you to swim the 50 in no less than 60 seconds.

Oh, gee. Okay, that shouldn't be too hard. Guess what? It IS!

Seems that between Tim's initial lessons with Doug, Owen and Jordan tweaking and suggesting refinements to my stroke and kicks and form, and now four ½ hour sessions with Mia I am actually swimming more efficiently, more powerfully and going faster than imagined. My intention was to swim the 50 yards in about 1:03, instead I came in at 57.1.

Mia says, "this time try to swim in 57 seconds."

I only modestly adjust my stroke and speed but now my time is 51.4, I am barely winded. Less than two weeks before I was killing myself for 49.91. HOW IS IT POSSIBLE to feel like I have taken a walk in the park with my time being barely 1.5 seconds different?

Mia says her mom's wisdom comes into play—'sometimes you have to slow down to go faster.'

Again, I discover unknown abilities within myself. I am blessed to have yet another amazing coach ever so gently guiding my new athleticism. Had I decided to simply stick to what I have known, not stepped outside of my comfort zone to learn something brand new, these accomplishments might never have been realised.

Six weeks after I had my last session with Mia I got back in the pool with Tim and his stop-watch. Tim had not really seen me swim since July when he turned my swim education over to Doug. Admittedly, and perhaps erroneously, I had given my writing precedence over my swimming (and fitness) goals.

Maybe the break was something my body needed. Maybe the voices of encouragement from Mia, Owen and Doug (formally as coaches) and Michele, Anna, Chelsea, Sue, Jordan, Brian, Scott, Mollie, Maggie and Kyle (informally as coaches but definitely cheerleaders) were resonating within me as I faced down the watch and my own negligence. All I know is that each component of my freestyle effort, the awareness of my body in the water as well as where I needed to do a 'certain thing' to get to the wall, my breathing, stroke, kick, flip turn, shimmer all came into me as some kind of astonishingly coordinated muscle memory. The net result of my first timed 50 (for speed) in more than two months was just shy of a second better than my personal best captured late in August with Doug (49.9) at 49.15 seconds. Moments later I managed to pull everything together and slice more than two seconds off that original personal best to realise 46.84 for my 50 yards. What? A hiatus from swimming and I have just clocked a time 3:06 seconds faster?

I text Owen away at school and get a "Whattt 46.8!!!! That's awesome I'm remarkably impressed" in reply.

As I write this I can't know whether I will make it to my self-imposed goal of 43 seconds by Thanksgiving Day. It certainly seems impossible to clear another four seconds off 50 yards in less than four weeks' time. When I think about losing 3.06 seconds in less than twenty minutes a few hours previous I have a new respect for what my body is capable of as well as having a renewed resolve to try.

11 chocolate yoga

Christmastime 2004 my neighbor Steve had never (shockingly EVER) cut down his own a Christmas tree. I invited him to help me cut down mine (his Volvo© sedan would make it much easier to cart a tree on top than my convertible). He drove, and then slogged through three feet of snow for nearly two hours with me until I found a perfect, 13' tall beauty. The tree variety smelled both of pine and citrus, yummy. I gave him my bow-saw (an estate sale find for $1 is hard to argue with when you insist on cutting your own tree each year) and some modest instructions, less than two inches into the trunk he cut himself, okay, let me have it back. Eventually we let the tree-lot staff takeover with the chain saw as I was getting soaked to the skin lying on the ground! The next day he sits on the hardwood floor of my kitchen, the mixing bowl from my KitchenAid© in his lap, spatula in hand, tackling the remainder of my hazelnut cheesecake batter as if he was five years old, not past fifty. All of this serves as a perfect example of 'chocolate yoga.'

You all should have more than a passing familiarity with chocolate; and I don't mean simply a Hershey© Bar or a Reese's© Peanut Butter Cup (though my friends Mia and Anna would argue that there is no greater pleasure to be had than the seasonal delights to be found in Reese's Peanut Butter Pumpkins!). Chocolate is as much about the comfort found in steaming hot chocolate with marshmallows as it is about stretching your taste buds around Mole sauce (okay, not my personal favourite), a gelato spiked with cayenne and roasted chili peppers and cinnamon or melting into the depth of a flourless chocolate cake.

Yoga is not, should not be, about the purely superficial tone, fun and fit mania adapted by Western Society—originally it was about mindfulness; a physical practice designed to achieve calm, focused attention and hopefully, a means of achieving *at-one-ment* with the Divine.

Now, what if you applied the original purposes of yoga, that is to say achieving a level of mindfulness, to 'eating' not just chocolate but also life? This is exactly how I live.

Late in August I was just about to start writing this chapter, when my girlfriend Bonnie sent me a parcel of over-the-top couture chocolate sustenance. She's done this 'surprise and delight' thing previously without reason or warning. As she had no idea I was even writing a book, there's no way she could have known about my efforts to define the sublime pleasure which comes to us from our sense of taste (or any other of our senses). In other words, her timing was perfect! Bonnie is very likely the only person (obviously, no longer) who understands my affinity for small portions of perfection as offered in the exquisite brands of Maribelle,© Voges© and Neuhaus.© In this case three small, perfectly crafted boxes of hand-made toffee, organic peanut butter, and marshmallow confections covered in Voges chocolate arrived packed with dry ice, eco-friendly air puffs, not so eco-friendly foam and a cardboard box large enough to hold 6 Magnums of Champagne. I thought not only about the pleasure each morsel would bring me but how each time I imbibe Bonnie will be giving me an encouraging hug to continue writing.

A couple of years ago I bought my girlfriend Jenn, a long ago bulimic, 12 bars of Scharffen-Berger© dark milk chocolate bars with toasted cacao nibs for her birthday. This was not, I might add, a thoughtless effort in any way intended to disregard all the pain she'd gone through in her recovery but rather to gently coax her along (with two of her three kids Griffin then age 3 and Hannah age 9) the path to the sensual pleasures to be derived from eating exquisitely. We sat outside on a warm day where letting the chocolate melt on your tongue was going to be less difficult than getting it into your mouth in a solid piece. Within a half an hour the kids were higher than kites on caffeine and sugar, chocolate moustaches (and fingers and cheeks) and smiling with pure joy. Hannah fully embraced the exercise of 'learning to eat chocolate' in turn by layering fresh strawberries or dried cherries on top to discover how the chocolate took on different characteristics depending upon the flavour paired with it. So enthusiastic in her exercises she asked at the end of the third bar if there was anymore (thankfully mom had hid the balance)!

I know that some readers will disagree with me on this point but, truly, it's not all about chocolate.

For me, not a crazed gourmand I assure you, the sensuality of food is no different than appreciating a cool evening breeze scented with butterfly bush, mimosa or jasmine. The practical needs of nourishment being realised before dawn by heading to the Farmer's Market for my eggs and honey, local fruits to eat fresh out of hand or to make jam or crumbles from, to collect my veggies and, occasionally, treat myself to a bouquet of fragrant

Casa Blanca lilies and gerbera daisies in shades of red to adorn my living room. It's the sound of bird song or of water cascading from a bronze fountain in a town square, the feel of silk or cashmere or French terrycloth lined sweatshirts against the skin. Being tactilely aware is no different than developing skills at arithmetic or becoming a world class cellist (though honing all of these skills takes patience, practice and passionate dedication).

In *The Spell of the Sensous*© David Abram speaks of his transformation of awareness as a result of the natural world around him opening up:

> . . . *I learned to notice the ray of sunlight that was then pouring through a chink in the roof, illuminating a column of drifting dust, and to realize that the column of light was indeed a power, influencing the air currents by its warmth, although I had not consciously seen it before, it had already been structuring my experience. My ears began to attend, in a new way, to the songs of birds—no longer just the melodic background to human speech, but meaningful speech in its own right, responding to and commenting on events in the surrounding earth.*

In reading that passage I fully recognised that the gift I have held precious for so long of cooing to doves and their nearly immediate like response and talking to bunnies and their not fleeing in fright, of somehow being intimate with new snow falling from a fir tree branch with the tiniest touch wasn't my unique experience, at least one other person in the world 'got it.' Living with this much awareness makes every day an endless possibility of experiences to be shared like Snow White© with her dwarfs.

Air to breathe is, just as my passion for being in the water, like the Philosophers' Stone. Why do we all seem to take for granted that both air and water will always just be available in abundance? If it's about to rain the air will shift directions bringing a freshness with it that borders on something magical—if only you leave yourself open to it.

I remember driving to my grandmother's house in Niagara Falls as a very little girl. There was a point as you exited the highway and turned onto Pine Avenue that the smells from the chemical plants on either side of the street assaulted my nose, eyes and taste buds. It was truly horrible. I used to survive by making a game of taking a huge breath and holding as long as I could so I wouldn't have to take another breath until we passed through the noxious cloud. But experiencing that onslaught taught me at a very tender age just how precious breathing air sweet with promised snow or rain could be.

I remember a very wild storm pressing down on the 300+ year old hotel I was staying at in Invermoriston, Scotland. The thick stone walls plus the very sensible siting (back of the inn built with 8 feet of a very steep mountain to buffer the weather) meant though I could hear the gale outside, but even with my windows open I couldn't catch a breeze.

In contrast, when I first lived in San Diego I was hosted on a rather lovely sailboat in one of its state rooms. The smell of dense, dampness from the salt air, the lulling sound of water lapping at the wooden hull, the boat tugging against its mooring and answering the tides made sleep a series of breath-taking discoveries each night, though the idea of camping under the stars holds not one bit of charm for me.

My current domicile is a one bedroom apartment in a building completed in 1929—before things fell apart (the last time). The steam heat works so well that I actually had my landlord install new radiator dials so I can turn them completely off. In the summer I die a little each degree higher the thermometer climbs, as much as I need fresh air it seems I need it to also be cold air! AC is my best summertime evening friend. Even in the dead of winter, snow piling up outside, sub-zero temperatures prevailing, will find my bedroom window open. I simply can't sleep in a closed up room—I need air moving around my face even as I bury myself under a down comforter tucked inside duvet, sheets, a thick wool blanket, a quilted blanket cover, and sometimes with a mohair throw over all to keep in my body heat. I burrow like a small animal, a 'breathing hole' sustaining me with clean deliciously cold air. Some of you are reading this thinking 'what about the flu and colds and bronchitis?' The truth is we should all open the house we live in up every day for fifteen minutes to remove allergens and dust mites and infections 'just waiting to happen.' Maybe this is the reason I rarely get sick. I have never had a flu shot. My lot in life seems to be that I am good for a three day bout of a chicken-soup-chills-and-fever-need-NyQuil™-and-menthol-scented-Puffs™ once every four years or so.

Open the windows all around the room. Turn off the lights. Put a pillow under your head, close your eyes. Smell the darkness. Breathe until you can really feel the room and your presence in it. If you are lucky at this point the air currents will waft across your face (just like that dog with its head out the car window). How can I describe the simple but powerful pleasure of this? Especially for those of you racing even to relax? I think it's like butterfly kisses—those delightful gifts children bestow using their tiny eyelashes when they first discover how happy it makes them (and the recipient) to 'kiss' this way.

I grew up less than ¾ of a mile from the upper rapids of the Niagara River which soon enough joins hundreds of millions of gallons of precious water cascading over the brink of Niagara Falls. It would be logical to assume that shuttling tourists around these waters for three years, in combination of growing up in view of the rising mists, would make me immune to awe and wonder. Quite the contrary, I think it made me more able to stand in a state of reverence. I am perfectly capable of attributing erosion and natural science to geology but when shafts of sunlight pierce clouds, streaming golden ribbons down to Earth I am completely lost to the idea that God is extending His Almighty hand gracing someone, somewhere.

Maulbronn in Baden-Württemberg, Germany, UNESCO World Heritage site, built in 1147 AD as an imperial abbey during the Holy Roman Empire remains the largest and most complete Cistercian monastery in Europe with its original fortifications still surrounding the complex.

I was on my knees of the main church, my reverence perhaps more complete as it was Christmas time. The space virtually devoid of any additional human presence, my breath coming in frosted wisps (heat? are you kidding?), and because Medieval European culture—all of it—is so very fascinating to me, I would almost swear to hearing the strains of long ago issued Gregorian chants of Compline resonating through the sanctuary. On my desk is cut-work sterling over red glass frame with a photograph I took laying backwards across the pew of the very center of the ceiling of the cloister. The image captures the still vibrant nearly 900 year old paint colours of deep red, gold, cobalt and cerulean blue decorating every convergence of the roofs' supporting stonework frame. Regardless of what God you worship, or the scope of your tolerance for faith in general, you must give credit that mankind's ability to erect beauty in the name of the Almighty transcends religious moniker. The picture has the ability to take me back to both the sacred beauty as well as the feeling of gratitude which spread through me developing into a silent cascade of tears so powerful that I wished only to prostrate myself before the high altar until emptied of my transcendence. Like so many gifts given when adequate thanks are offered, my blessings expanded as I exited the church to the right of the altar, passing the ancient choir and entering a connecting hallway running behind the nave. To the upper right at the ceiling eave was a trefoil window (three roundels of glass). By all logic and applicable laws of light fragmentation any sunbeam coming through this window should have cast a clover shaped pattern on the medieval stones. It did not. It absolutely cast an image of a cross. I recall looking up at the window in an attempt to comprehend that what I was seeing on the floor was 'real' and somehow not an optical illusion. There was no explanation to the connection between the architecture of the window and what I was seeing. The stark contrast of golden light and dark stone virtually ensured that when the film (not digital) was developed it would 'prove' what I had seen. I took two frames and in both instances the cross on the floor was clearly visible through my viewfinder. Rather, the developed images showed absolutely nothing but flagstones worn smooth by the footsteps of eight and a half centuries of novices, monks, pilgrims and caretakers. Why, following my 'great blessing of tears,' would I be foolish enough to even attempt to document the Divine, the omnipotent presence of God? Because just as visitors to Medjugorje swear they see apparitions of the Virgin Mary and smell roses where none bloom we want, perhaps need, to believe beyond experience with something clasp to our breast as evidence.

To stand in a place next to the sea where 5000 years of human habitation has taken place is humbling. It is, I think, I perfectly natural thing to issue forth a silent prayer of gratitude for being able to come to Scara Brae in the Orkney Islands. As I did so large, really large, raindrops flung themselves out of a cloudless, bright blue, sun-filled sky. In this natural amphitheatre formed by ocean and land, connecting the contemporary houses to my far right and the subterranean Neolithic ones just to my left along the path from the parking lot and visitor centre, a double rainbow formed in front of me. My companion, an Orkney native, turned to stare at me in disbelief.

. . . God, who richly provides us with everything for our enjoyment.
—1 Timothy 6:17

My connection with God is not like tasting chocolate or practicing yoga, it's much more. We need to understand that sensuous pleasure is not about control, but relinquishing it to partake in all the goodness that God has created for us to enjoy.

When I was in third grade I wanted to be a nun. The idea of dedicating my life to doing God's work was infinitely appealing. Then, I discovered boys. Intellectually I might not have understood why the two weren't necessarily compatible but on some intuitive level I certainly did.

My spirit revisited the idea of Divine service post 9/11, more earnestly, when I applied to Episcopal Divinity School in Cambridge, MA for their Doctorate of Comparative Religion program. I got through the application process and down to the interviews; five candidates for two slots. Maybe showing up in my 'uniform' of mules, sarong, red lipstick, French-cuffed blouse and cufflinks didn't quite gel with my interviewers' perception of what an ordained Episcopal priest should look like. More likely is my interpretation of Jesus' life which aligns nicely with Jewish and Muslim and Buddhist traditions but not-so-much with being a Christian.

I truly embrace the concept that there is only one God and His will be done on Earth as it is in Heaven, but it's the Prophet part that continues to hang me up. That, and the two natures of God, the wars fought between Shi'as and Sunni, Christians and Jews, Muslims and Christians, Catholics against Copts, Jews and Muslims, Muslims and Buddhists, Hindu and Buddhists, Protestants and Catholics slugging it out for 'who's right' domination (okay, maybe the Buddhists aren't part of the global domination feeding frenzy). If we're all God's children then why can't we play nice in the sandbox together? (I am being rhetorical. I have studied all of the dynamics sufficiently to understand.)

Perhaps if we were more confident in our individual beliefs we wouldn't be so threatened by ones at odds with our own. For all that has been wrought in God's name self-righteousness is the least understandable to me. I can't bring myself to believe that one person's interpretation of God is better than another—especially with hypocrisy so rampant, especially when there is so much suffering that could be offset with mutual respect and cooperation.

What you do speaks so loud that I cannot hear what you say.
— Ralph Waldo Emerson

Regardless of what their story might be when we get off the Mass Pike at Newton and exit toward Cambridge they stand there waiting; men line up 30 yards apart on either side of the ramp panhandling. Drivers waiting for the light, at the high end well over $100,000 and at the low, faded paint, fenders flapping and sometimes with duct tape holding the car together, are joined in the same discomfort and human misery so aptly pointed out by Phil Collins in his eighties hit Another Day in Paradise©. Rarely have I ever seen someone put down their window and hand over the equivalent of a gallon of gas or Starbucks© latte to even one of the four to six homeless men trying to hold themselves together in this ancient way.

I don't endorse turning over cash which might wind up passing over the counter in a liquor store or to a drug dealer at some playground; I have come to embrace something else. My gesture is almost completely anonymous, as it should be. When I travel this route I have sitting on the front passenger seat a small bag of fresh fruit that I buy just before heading out. Somehow handing someone thin as a stick an apple or orange, a pear, banana or even a drink coupon is like metaphorically inviting them to join me at the dining room table. Here. Nourish yourself. But for the grace of God, and amazing friends, it could be me standing there in your place.

It's something insignificant against the totality of the global hunger problem. In the United Kingdom an estimated 4 million people go hungry. Yet, because it's less problematic than figuring out distribution channels some 17 million tons of perfectly usable foods wind up ploughed into landfills each year. In the United States, the average American family throws out 14% of their weekly food purchases which results in waste totalling approximately $600 annually. Do some simple math. There are 300 million people living in the United States, even if you discount the number of people living alone and 'assume' a household consists of four people that's $4.5B annually simply going to waste—in the United States alone. 14% of our grocery bill just thrown away!

How can we enjoy 'chocolate yoga' when others go hungry, live in polluted wastelands, still have to carry drinking and cooking water from wells miles away? It's true none of us can fix everything, but there's a very real opportunity to quietly help address hunger with great compassion. I am not suggesting offering relief somewhere intellectually and emotionally disconnected from you, rather help people who live less than 10 miles from your own front door. What are you and yours reasonably going to eat in a week? Why not revise your grocery list a bit, ensure against spoilage and waste, then write a check on a quarterly basis for $100 to your local food bank?

12 gypsy

Recently, and for the first time in nearly thirty years of our acquaintance, I walked into the business of a gentleman I know to be greeted with, "Hey, the gypsy is here!" I might not have thought very much about it save for the fact that at the time of writing this book I have developed a serious case of wanderlust. Again.

I am probably the only single, straight woman on the planet who owns her own considerable pile of padded moving blankets. I break down, fold flat and then hoard the heavy cardboard boxes I have found for moving my fine art. You see I haven't, since my divorce in 1991, stayed in any one place for very long and these accoutrements are quite necessary to surviving what most people take on less than five times in the course of their lives. That expressed, I recognise that I really am getting too old to help moving guys lift all my furniture up and down flights of staircases, and onto and off of trucks to ensure none of it is dropped and that it is properly placed to avoid damage in transport. Ideally it would all be crated but that's totally unrealistic given the limitations of my storage spaces and the (up to now) perpetual lack of depth to my wallet. I have been in my current domicile for nearly four years—aside from childhood, a record. I feel the urge for a change of scenery keenly, stuck in a city that feels too small without space to properly breathe. A city, which because I am not really 'from here' and where I have no significant history, despite now having family and a long list friends in the immediate vicinity isn't where I want to be. Not that I know whatever/wherever is next but I surely hope the location fulfills every sensibility and precludes any other relocation—ever.

I find it rather amusing that I own a nearly life size metaphor for the transient aspect of my life, an extraordinary oil painting of a gypsy woman. Her resemblance so striking to my own that when my mother saw the painting for the first time she said, 'when did you have your portrait painted?' Aside from the minor offense taken at being thought to be in possession of sufficient vanity, where would I get the finances and how would I justify the expense? I didn't. I swear. A couple of male friends have commented over the years that it's a little spooky having a conversation with me and having her stare at them—questioning their presence and designs.

Any one that has ever walked into a room and experienced a sense of 'been-here, done-that' déjà vu will relate. I have never done past life regression to discover the connections we might share but there is surely something 'there' currently hanging above my mantelpiece.

I don't know who she is. Hers was a second canvas found beneath the one actually desired from an estate auction in Cleveland. She was painted in Paris in 1922 by an American woman. She is appears to be in her twenties, assuming she survived WWII she would have been close to seventy at the time of my birth in 1961.

The first time I saw her I felt sick to my stomach, same thing on every subsequent viewing. Why would any sane (modestly questionable) person go out of their way to buy a painting that makes them queasy? I can only explain this as she felt like a part of me hanging on that gallery wall and needed to be reunited with me and my life. When I finally brought her home the sick-to-my-stomach feeling ceased, abruptly.

I fully recognise that I am (currently) a slave to my possessions and especially to this alter bit of my person. She is usually left on the wall until last. Gently padded with the clean cotton bath rugs and then wrapped in a vintage Hudson Bay© blanket before she is tucked behind the seats of my car to be moved with my various instant kitchen, bedroom and bathroom boxes.

I am of the opinion that everyone 'needs' a singular albatross that defines and maybe anchors them to this life until such a time as our mortal flesh becomes irrelevant.

Regardless of its level of preciousness what 'thing' (people count in a totally different way and are not in this category) could you simply not live without?

13 and so to bed!

As **I see it** there's no separation between the potential delight to be found in life's experiences while asleep and those to be found when awake. In other words, hedonism knows no bounds.

The essential element to living in the moment, passionately aware and fully engaged is . . . sleep. We all approach sleep differently. No way is right or wrong as long as you are comfortable. I won't suggest to any of you reading this that my obsession is right for you. (I promise this chapter has nothing to do with addressing sleep apnea.)

I am from Western New York, decidedly a modest middle class background, growing up with hand-me-down furniture in my bedroom. My undoing, if it can be considered that, as it relates to my bedroom and specifically my bed can be traced to having a job at 17 with a carriage trade retailer with a linen department on the basement level. It does something to the psyche of a teenage girl accustomed to heavy 100% cotton white muslin (read 'practical') sheets to see those tiny mock beds perfectly made up every couple of weeks with a new pattern of breath-taking prettiness, a mountain of plush pillows and a throw, luxuriously draped at the end. I was surely doomed from the beginning.

First order of business was squirreling away money to buy a glorious set of deep royal blue sheets with a self-fabric ruffled hem strewn with red roses called Guinevere—yes, incredibly, 35 years later I still remember the pattern name. Next up, a set of white sheets, cases, shams and dust ruffle with a 6-inch wide eyelet border for my hope chest—while I was generations passed the 'bride comes with a trousseau' I was charmed by the idea and relentless in my acquisitions. In retaliation for some trivial sibling dispute my brother ratted-me-out to the parents. You'd think I had dope under my bed! I was commanded to bring them out from hiding and show them to my parents. I recall my father saying, "No self-respecting man will be caught dead sleeping on those . . ." (Funny, years later my newly-wed husband had absolutely no issue with them saying, 'they make you happy and I am just going to close my eyes anyway.')

Any collection is madness, but at least mine I get to use every day. I freely admit to being a 'sheet whore'—so obsessed about sleeping on beautiful bed linens that I have driven eight hours to the (now defunct) Anichini© outlet stores in White River Junction, Vermont, and West Lebanon, New Hampshire, for their annual clearance sale. I built a linen closet to accommodate my collection and then organise them by season.

Like most everyone else, I have a bed and I put these sheets on it. Unlike 90% of the population my bed and its linens are, I admit, a little over the top. To put this into perspective I once had a radiator spewing water all over my bedroom carpet, and the side of my headboard. Desperate, I called my friend Kevin (whose work schedule was flexible enough for a mid-afternoon intervention) to come over and help me move the bed—it weighs a ton normally requiring three people to handle the headboard when it's set up or taken apart—so we could lift the rug and take it outside to dry. Kevin got as far as my bedroom door, stopped dead in his tracks and said, "Whoa, a guy's gotta be pretty serious to go in there."

Oh Kevin, please, JUST HELP ME MOVE IT!!

It's almost as if my collection paved the way for the bed to be found. How I came to own this treasure is impossibly unlikely but is as much about believing that if something is truly meant to be, anything can happen. Equally so, it's also about appreciation and, I believe, expressing it out loud.

Honestly, the sheer pleasure of simply viewing, running my hands along the Carpathian walnut surfaces, marvelling at the craftsmanship and bronze d'Or mounts of flower garlands, bow-knots, oak and laurel leaves, ostrich plume finials, and acanthus mouldings was enough. My bed was made as part of a 14 piece suite in Paris sometime in the 1920's. I can't imagine having a bedroom large enough to accommodate 14 pieces of furniture! Quite frankly all of it belonged in a museum someplace. Yet it was sitting in an antique shop in Hudson, NY. The absolute exquisiteness of it beyond 'mere mortals' being worthy of owning it, that, and the $56,000.00 price tag for the group, made the potential purchase not even a remote possibility.

Beauty draws us back, time and again, to view art in museums, to walk along a sea shore at sunrise or sunset, to chase rainbows and butterflies, to watch as the final seconds in a soccer match tick down and a miraculous, perfectly made effort results in the winning goal. And so, over the course of 18 months, I kept finding excuses to drive to Hudson to 'visit' the bed and its companions—just to admire.

 109

On one occasion the store owners suggested they might be willing to sell the bed separately.

Really, but it's a suite, why would you separate it?

Whoever can afford the suite will want a king size bed.

Already knowing the price will be scary, I still hear myself ask, *"How much?"*

$5600.00 plus tax and delivery

Ouch. No, thank you. Do you mind if I come back to visit it again?

When you come from Western New York you just don't actually consider spending that kind of money for something to sleep in. A bed like that is faery tale stuff, like marrying a prince and living in a castle or winning the lottery in a very big way. Five or six months pass. Another visit, more verbal appreciation, more longing caresses. Sigh.

We'd consider a discount if the sale was paid in cash.

No, sorry, my company has been sold and I am looking for another job right now.

Leave Hudson and the bed, again.

In January of 1998 I land a 'dream job' I had been pursuing for four months allowing me to move to Boston. I have made a 30% leap in my salary from my previous role just as my unemployment was about to run out. Whew. Four months later I call the antique dealers.

Is there any chance you still have the bed?

Yes, we do.

III

What, exactly, was the cash price you had in mind?

$4,000

Would the price be honoured if I sent it to you in two payments?

Yeah, we'd do that for you.

Why?

In our business the people who can really afford the prices of the best things rarely appreciate them. They buy them to impress but don't understand what went into making it. You do. We talked about the last time you were in. We put a SOLD tag on the bed when you left. We didn't know when, but we did know that you were the only person we were going to sell the bed to.

Oh My Gosh, are you kidding me? (and, yes, I cry tears of gratitude).

It cost another $500 to have it delivered to Boston, but no tax as it was crossing state lines.

The ultimate justification for its purchase came as a result of the fact that I don't have a daily latte Jones. Nor do I smoke, I rarely go out to dinner, and up to that point in my life my vacations had always spent with my parents at their home 'being helpful.' The amortized cost per day for a year came out $12.32 but I figured if I lived to 80 then (with a great grandfather that remarried in his eighties I have a pretty good shot at this) the cost per day would go down to less than 30 cents. The sheer overwhelming beauty of this bed being mine for a mere thirty-cents-a-day, the privilege of spending 30% of the remainder of my life sleeping in it, how could I not buy the bed?

The things we own do not inherently have meaning. Really, they don't. Being human means we have the ability to assign value to what we regard as important—but all of it is transient in nature: a sand castle, a child's drawing, a love letter, a card from a long ago occasion are treasured precisely as Elizabeth Taylor said of her collection of precious 'bling,' "The importance of jewelry is emotional and psychological. Nobody ever owns anything this beautiful . . ." But, in adding her own provenance to the storied history of these extraordinary pieces, Miss Taylor's collection comes to a role far superior to that of gracing one of the worlds' most beautiful women—auctioned by Christie's in late 2011 to the considerable benefit of The Elizabeth Taylor AIDS Foundation. The real value of owning something 'precious' is that at the end of our enjoyment good work might be done from its sale. I am fully cognizant that, though ludicrous to compare to Ms Taylor's jewels, I don't really own this magnificent bed. I am merely its present day care-taker and in exchange for ensuring its longevity I get to sleep in it.

In a world of easy care, and T-shirt material sheets there is nothing to compare with the pure, sensual pleasure of freshly pressed Egyptian cotton. Unless of course you are amongst those individuals who can afford to send your linens to the dry cleaners or French laundry I am sure the idea of using heavy spray starch to iron the hem turnover, cases and shams is making your head spin. For two nights each week my bed looks as though it was part of a spread in *Architectural Digest*© but only a handful of people will ever see it.

The first night, climbing in between crisp, silky smooth, perfectly scented (with organic botanicals from glycerine soaps tucked between each layer in the linen closet) sheets into my bed is nothing short of experiencing some measure of heaven on earth.

Over the years I have painstakingly amassed a room around it to complement its beauty. I heaped my sweaters and lingerie in old wicker picnic baskets for years until I found a 18th century marble topped (original) mahogany bureau built as Napoléon was marching toward Waterloo in Boston—thankfully securing it as a container was about to arrive at less than 1/3 of the price it had been six months earlier. From Middlebury, Ridgefield and Greenwich, CT, I found the vases and candlesticks and lampshades that were turned into very pretty lamps. My great, great-grandmother's carved ivory and silk parasol, now shadowboxed on silk within a heavy gold leafed frame along with a collection of 19th century hand coloured botanicals lithographs in shades of blues and lavenders matted on mottled lavender with Italian marbled papers and blue inked lines, a monolith of a beach-scape of St. Albans and very early Oriental period pastel called Jerusalem's Gate grace the pale lavender walls and a stunning, if not authentically Persian, hand-knotted Sino-Tabriz in silk and wool. Every single choice was patient and deliberate, very personal, meaningful for the chase, location found or who might have been along for the shared the experience leading up to the acquisition.

As much as I notice every tiny thing of beauty around me, this bed which has come together by chance, serendipity and pure aesthetic appreciation, where I can renew myself each night to face the next day is darn close to being something sacred to me.

When you go to bed tonight be mindful of the scent of your room, the lighting, the feel of your skin against your sheets, the softness of the pillow cradling your head, the weight of the blankets or comforter, the temperature of the room, and if applicable, hopefully most of all, the scent of your partner lying beside you and how warm (or cold) their feet are as your toes reach theirs. I wish you sweet dreams.

14 stuff

Happiness resides not in possessions, and not in gold, happiness dwells in the soul.
—Democritus, 460–370 BC

. . . then drive over to Wal-Mart, watch them piling up the crap, stuff they didn't need, stuff they didn't even want, stuff they'd throw in the closet, then buy a bigger house for more closet space, more room to pile up more stupid fucking crap.
—The Hired Gun, Matthew Branton, 2001

I had already framed out my own sentiments about stuff when I read Matthew Branton's The Hired Gun in the summer of 2011. His characters' diatribe resonated so strongly with me I had to catch my breath. He clearly 'gets it'—a writer is rather like the rest of us being under the influence of alcohol; the truth, our core beliefs, tend to come out through the characters on the page. What's odd to me is that Mr Branton owns homes in both London and on the big island of Hawaii, presumably finding balance to his financial well-being by adhering to his passion for skateboarding and surfing when he isn't writing.

The equivalent of California Closets© wasn't likely to have enjoyed market penetration in the ancient world—Jimmy Choo's© not yet being all the rage. But, as is evident by Democritus' words man and woman have had a noteworthy obsession with amassing things for more than 2400 years. Even as pre-Christian Greeks relentlessly pursued possessions, the same erroneous belief continues to prevail along Michigan Avenue, Rue du Faubourg Saint-Honoré or the local big box store, such as Walmart.© Democritus identified no matter how much we own, no matter what scale of physical beauty or rarity which can be assigned to the item, regardless of the gold, or stocks and bonds or size or number of homes, in the end it's all 'just stuff.' The value of these things does not validate the individual. As we amass wealth and fill up the spaces around us with possessions, happiness will not come into our lives if it isn't already in our hearts.

After reading this you probably will think I live as minimally as a monastic cell or in a spare, even austere, ultra-modern space—not a chance.

When I was a very little girl my parents became friends with a childless couple who came to be known to my brother and I as Aunt Dorothy and Uncle Al. Aunt Dorothy was a tall, shift dress wearing woman with a dramatic upsweep chignon hairdo held in place with mountains of hair pins and volumes of hair spray. Whenever we were together she always held my tiny 5 year-old hand in one of her own incredibly soft ones, long fingers adorned with an array of large carat weight semi-precious and precious stones including amethysts, smoky topaz and citrines. She and Uncle Al owned the top producing sire of champion Cocker Spaniels in the country. They also owned a trucking firm and an antiques business which they ran out of a log cabin on their expansive property in Chardon, Ohio. With all the material wealth they possessed they were charming, down-to-earth people who were very comfortable in their own skin.

I remember the magic I found in the rooms in which they lived. In retrospect I recognise that Aunt Dorothy had truly exquisite things but she didn't treat anything as 'museum precious.' Thick hand-knotted Persian carpets, a velvet sofa in stripes of blue, red, green and gold, a hand-carved, bejeweled, wooden carousel horse complete with horse-hair mane, forelock and tail on a red and white striped pole was mounted floor to ceiling next the fireplace. A small vitrine held ancient bronze, ivory and jade Buddha's. For all this, and more, if you turned an object over it always had a price tag on it. She enjoyed her collections with pleasure for the time allotted their ownership but easily let these lovely things pass through her life. Aunt Dorothy made gifts to me of Geisha dolls made entirely of silk and mounted on ebony bases. Uncle Al 'sold' me my first antique at age five for $1, a children's tea set in pink soft paste porcelain with gilded rims made in Germany. When we stopped at their home after a dog show we'd share buckets of Kentucky Fried Chicken© and Pepperidge Farm© chocolate layer cake with white frosting. She absolutely leveled a waitress at The Brown Derby© one night because instead of bringing me the fresh fruit salad I ordered (on a ½ pineapple) the woman delivered a footed cup with industrial canned fruit cocktail complete with over-dyed Maraschino cherries. The lesson unintentionally imparted upon me was to speak-up if something is wrong and you don't get what you ordered. I embrace this a little more nicely than Aunt Dorothy did, but she was like a she-cat when it came to making me happy.

My paternal grandmother who was by no means wealthy distilled her own philosophy about the ownership of things to me when I was about 10. She was a testament to the old expression "A thing of beauty is a joy forever." In her more junior years she was the embodiment that it was infinitely better to possess one truly exquisite item than a house full of junk. Her philosophy was applied equally to the fabric and yarns she used for making clothing (she was an extraordinary seamstress and knitter), the ingredients for her cooking and baking (30 some varieties of cookies each Christmas), her fine, hand-painted porcelain china and her mahogany furniture—the tables which graced her living room my brother now uses in his library. She bought quality and then used it, took care of it and derived pleasure from it every day—whatever the 'it' might have been. Her house, like my maternal grandmother's, was neat as a pin. Their tidiness was not obsessive least you think they cleaned all day or had maids. I think it was influenced by the fact that they were born just before WWI broke out and came of age and married during the Great Depression. What little they had they wanted, even needed, to last. On a global basis no society embraced the concept of 'disposable' in those times. And yet, in less than two generations and 80 years the shift in our consuming habits has put our planet in peril.

I arrived in the Shetland Islands, Scotland well after dark to visit some of Thistle & Broom's fascinating octogenarian (they have experienced SO MUCH life) Fair Isle hand-knitters. By the time I retrieved my bag, collected the rental car and I completed my island hopping to arrive Rosabell's it was well after 9PM when we sat down to dinner. Rosabell was telling me about her family and one particular story struck a hard, dissonant chord, within me. She was speaking of her childhood, a time between WWI and WWII, "we didn't have much, but we always had enough."

Within days I was back in the States where Hummers© (the size of Rosabell's kitchen) were cutting me off, people were not-so-nicely waiting for ridiculously expensive cups of coffee, and the perpetual frenzy of contemporary American life threatened to swamp me. Suddenly David Abrams' *The Spell of The Sensuous* read years before had greater weight in my own psyche. His own research was grounded, literally, between Indonesian rice paddies and Nepalese mountains. Surrounded by incredible beauty, as I have repeatedly been exposed to in Scotland's wild spaces and modest homes, Mr Abrams connected to fire flies and shooting stars blurring the lines between above and below, the fullness of scent in places where cooking fires still glow and animals are husbanded nearby, the scents of life and decay in equal measure. Our antiseptic Western olfactory senses would rather isolate commercial farms pouring ridiculous quantities of industrial chemicals and farm effluents into the environment and pretend that this doesn't exist than live close to the land in harmony with indigenous livestock as my friends Minty and Aeneas Mackay have for the last 20 years—at this writing they have just sold their beloved Ardalanish Farm on the Isle of Mull and the new owners of Ann and Andrew Smith have taken on their legacy and stewardship.

For many of us the perfectly adequate closets, cupboards, attics and garages of our homes call to mind a Blondie© cartoon from the 1980's where Dagwood opens what appears to be a small, ordinary closet and the contents spill over him and bury him like an avalanche. Nearly thirty years later we still aren't satiated. Using Rosabell's family and my own grandmother as an examples, just how much is enough?

I think the manic purchasing is trying to fix some unseen hole in the soul. Self-worth, validation, respect (the list is endless) is not gained by brandishing the latest Louis Vuitton©️ or Hermes©️ handbag, Tiffany©️ jewelry or boxes arriving daily from QVC.©️ Just because you *can*, does that necessarily mean you should?

Please don't misunderstand me. Like my Aunt Dorothy and my most beloved girl-friend Doris who was also an antique dealer and remains a connoisseur of exquisite things, I have less than ordinary 'stuff.' I have a bad habit (read expensive) of rescuing things like Victorian chaise longues from winding up in the dump and bringing home antique glass Christmas ornaments.

To live with things often (far) older than 100 years is to accept the responsibility that I am but a temporary custodian. Running my hand over the French polish of a table, or holding a tiny, finely cast bronze Buddha in the palm of my hand is to be connected with all the previous owners of each piece and elicits a pleasure that a purchase from IKEA©️ will never.

I recall reading an editorial in the late 1970's by the then editor of shelter publication House Beautiful©️ JoAnn Barwick. She was relating a story about being a young editorial assistant and newly-wed trying awfully hard to overcome her perceived failings of the décor of her modest apartment with the imminent arrival of her very high profile, arbiter of taste, boss for dinner. I can't recall who the boss was, but even as a junior in high school I embraced the advice.

To paraphrase: Investment decorating isn't about owning the most precious things, it's about waiting to find things to purchase that you will love your whole life. Never be in a hurry, even if you can afford to, always have a plan.

As a result, it took me 23 years to 'finish' my living room. It brings me delight and offers my guests comfort. The pursuit of these possessions wasn't obsessive, everything has evolved as naturally as laugh lines or crow's feet do on our faces. My living room is like sitting in a Wedgewood© Jasperware teacup with crimson red and French blue fabrics softening the edges. No matter where I make my home the contents can fit into grand spaces or re-arrange nicely for in smaller, more intimate settings. I come home at the end of the day and sink into the down-filled seating and soothing colours with a sigh of relief.

My last purchase was the ultimate rescue and rehabilitation. In the chock-a-block environment of a commercial greenhouse being used to host an estate sale I was struck by one piece at the far side and end of it all. Almost forlornly sat a nearly wrecked piece of history, American Empire, likely made sometime around 1810 in New England, exquisite carved acanthus plinth, hairy carved Griffith feet finishing the tri-corn shaped base, round tilt top drum table with its original brass pin, solid and veneers of deeply grained mahogany. I could envision someone taking it home, spray painting it with Krylon© and letting their kids use it for crafts projects. Badly damaged from damp, veneers lifting or missing, cracks where they shouldn't be, its original brass feet long gone and rot deep within the base. It would take time, patience, incredible skill, and money I really didn't have to spend to stabilize and respectfully restore—not refinish—it. I measured to make sure it would fit in my currently smallish living-room. I photographed. I dragged friends out to see it to make sure I wasn't insane (they know otherwise). I researched the auction and retail prices of similar pieces scattered across the Eastern United States and Britain to place a limit on what I could justify spending in total. I called highly qualified old school furniture makers and one *ébéniste* (so called because the original mid-17th century French masters of the craft of veneering preferred working with ebony). It took me three days to talk myself into taking on this project and successfully negotiating the price downward to under $300 plus a 20+ mile delivery. It took five months and four times the amount I paid for it to do the work including French polishing. The table now serves as my desk and dining table and it is gorgeous. Assuming any of us are still here, my Empire table is ready to face another two hundred years to provide pleasure with dignity.

I do not live in a roped off museum, my nieces languish and we eat on 19th century painted tray tables, melted chocolate stains the silk damask of my sofa.

Half my kitchen is exactly the shade of green of bright new ivy leaves, the other is bright white. I have a red microwave, a bejeweled mermaid wall clock, and the kitchen art is a collection of event posters from around the world beautifully framed making a gallery of my life (like big girl refrigerator art). My bathroom vivid with an outrageous ruffled shower curtain which Monet could have painted as an abstract and a pair of watercolours bought in Paris rendered in shades of vermilion, yellow, coral, touches of blues, green and translucent purples. It would make most people insane to live in such a kaleidoscope, honestly I find it reassuring.

I have been blessed to know antique dealers whose own passions for beauty have suggested deposits and prolonged payment plans allowing me to become the owner of some truly astonishing things. All of which are likely to be sold long before I have to think about executing a last will and testament. Why? Because like my Aunt Dorothy and girlfriend Doris I recognise at the end of the day it is all still just 'stuff' and to anyone I love the ownership of these things would be an enormous burden. In the meantime the patina, textures, warmth of nearly ancient (against mainstream sensibilities) finishes brings me immeasurable pleasure for the beauty I live with day in and day out.

I am not suggesting you embrace any of this in your home but maybe some outrageously thick, jewel-toned bath towels could be worked in? Perhaps before you head out to your local furniture store to replace that less-than-five-year-old sofa, think about hitting a store which carries excellent quality vintage and antique furniture. You'll likely be very surprised just how much further your money will go toward owning something comfortable and well-made that is already a bit more than half century old. Finally, a great upholsterer can transform your 'new' old find into something uniquely yours instead of something that looks like it could belong to any one of your neighbors.

15 pebble in the pond

When I was in 1st grade I needed an emergency appendectomy. To this day I can recall the searing pain on my right side as I walked from my classroom to the nurse's office. Less than four hours later I was in surgery—the doctors removed it just before my appendix would have ruptured. When I woke up post recovery in my room there was this amazing flower arrangement next to my bed. It looked like an old fashioned ice cream soda, like in Norman Rockwell paintings, peppermint striped and white carnations, a couple of red and white (paper) straws bent for 'sipping' in a tall 'soda glass' vase. It was from my 1st grade teacher Mrs Dwyer.

Mrs Dwyer valued me in a way that left an indelible impression on the psyche of a scared, sick, six-year old little girl. When I came home she was there again, a huge Easter basket accompanied her. As a result to this day I still get excited about the first appearance of marshmallow Peeps weeks before Easter each year (yellow only and by the way they really are better if you let the outsides get 'just a little' dry so when you bite into them they crunch). At year's end, my gift to her was a silver-coloured heart-shaped hinged metal box lined in red velvet. It wasn't something my parents paid for, I used my 25-cents-a-week allowance to save up to buy it.

In the 3rd grade Mrs Dwyer continued to enrich my life—and the wardrobe of my Barbie™ dolls! A raspberry pink corduroy marabou trimmed cape, a garden party dress of pale yellow dotted Swiss trimmed with yellow and white daisy appliques, a spectacular lace wedding gown complete with a tiara of seed pearls and a tulle veil. I think back on those incredible hand stitched clothes now and recognise that had they been adult sized they were worthy of any French couturier. I know that in today's society this will strike the more cynical among you as an odd extension of the teacher/student relationship, maybe it was better growing up in the 1960's!

At 23 I married, Mrs Dwyer (along my elementary school principal Miss Catherine DiVizio) was in the church. As my husband Stephen and I were pronounced man and wife, it was Mrs Dwyer (not my parents or his) decked out in three shades of pink with a hat embellished in pink marabou who bolted out of her pew to kiss us both and give us her blessing. She impacted my taste in decorating in my living in a way that I didn't connect until many years later—I have an occasional chair that belonged to my grandmother that I refinished and then had upholstered in a hand printed cream chintz festooned with red and white and red carnations from Cowton & Tout. It's probably quite obvious that I still love her very much. Mrs Dwyer remarried in her 80's and went hiking in the Himalayas on her honeymoon. Somehow Julie Armstrong's ascent of Mount Kilimanjaro and Diana Nyad's momentous swim seem tame in contrast to a woman resembling Mrs Claus doing a great adventure in the Himalayas at 83.

Her love for me serves as a perfect example of what Mr Meredith, my 7th grade social studies teacher, called "The Pebble in The Pond" theory.

I wonder if any of any of Mr Meredith's hundreds of students hung onto his philosophy for more than 10 minutes let alone have 'lived it' every day for nearly forty years. Mr Meredith was a physically imposing man, over 6' tall, barrel chested, baritone voiced, grizzle bearded, half-moon bespectacled. He taught us history, geography and introduced us to thinking critically about current events and the role we might one day play in shaping our world. He was generous of spirit but a task-master. I think his greatest lesson was his Pebble in the Pond lecture.

 127

You stand at the edge of a pond. You throw a pebble in. After the splash, the ripples swirl out from the point of entry toward you—at which point, most people walk away. But if you stay, and watch, you'd discover that those ripples would actually come to the edge of the pond and then return to where the pebble went into the water in the first place.

Clearly, Mrs Dwyer remained in my life long enough to experience first-hand the net result of pitching her pebble of love into the pond of my tiny heart.

At 12 this was my initial introduction to 'for every action there is a like reaction' and it is also about the time I decided that I was going to live my life in a way that "left the room lighter than when I came into it." You are reading this and thinking 'At Twelve?' Why is it that adults tend to be surprised when a child exhibits wisdom? I really believe that as we age we actually un-learn universal knowledge, and it's a rare kid (sometimes now referred to as an 'Indigo Child') who almost miraculously manages to defy society and stay in this pure state.

So, perhaps this is as good as place as any to express that a couple years later *The Reincarnation of Peter Proud©* was released and it changed my (then short) life. Despite the fact that I was 14 and some of the subject matter could have been considered (at the time) a little too mature, I was allowed to see it. Funny how some things impact your whole belief system. Reincarnation made so much more sense to me than our physical bodies dying and our souls transcending to Heaven to commune with angels, other dead people, and the Holy Trinity.

Which is perhaps why when I met Hideo in Fort Lauderdale, Florida, in 2006 absolutely nothing he said to me came as a surprise.

Sensei Hideo Izumoto, 85 years young and a Shinto priest, had driven 10 hours to meet me. Okay, startling enough. Who wants any eighty-five-year-old driving 10 hours anywhere? But equally so, we'd had no previous contact. I didn't know a thing about his journey being part of my visit. And I was in the midst of cooking catfish, fried green tomatoes and making corn bread (I embrace the home-cooked food is love, affection, a hug for the insides philosophy of life) for the couple with whom I was staying. Blane, the husband, had come home, took one look at me covered with flour and grease and announced that Hideo would be here in a half hour. You can understand when you suddenly discover an elderly holy man has gone to such lengths to meet you, getting into the shower and getting cleaned up becomes a real priority. You don't ask to have the blanks filled in.

As Hideo is both Japanese and a holy man, and my considerable elder, my understanding of cultural protocol demanded that I bow very deeply to him. To my absolute shock, and embarrassment, his bow to me was a deep as my own. As he rises from his bow, he takes my hands in his own, looks me in the eye and says, "It's good to see you again my friend, it's been far too long." We have been standing in front of each other for less than a minute and I have no cognitive memory of ever having met this man before. Well, therein would be the critical point of our encounter but it would take me another three years before I was compelled to enquire how he knew that we knew each other.

I think it's to be understood that intellectually I still have a hard time grasping the implications of our being brother and sister in a previous lifetime—especially one, as he says, took place 31,000 years ago in Atlantis.

It's also a little disconcerting to be talked about as if you are not less than three feet away. The dialogue between Blane and Hideo went something like this:

Her energy is pure, white light.

Yes, with a slight lavender tint.

Everything she has been meant to accomplish will be finished in this life.

It's why I wanted you to meet her.

For the record, this was a bit more 'out there' than intellectually I had had to embrace previously. But hey! Aren't there more things in Heaven and Earth that we don't understand than science has discovered? As a result I am open to all of what the world brings to my door and there is clearly something in this meeting which I am supposed to embrace, pass on, witness, and challenge myself (or others) to learn from the world around me. Honestly, I still don't know if I am doing what Hideo and Blane (and others) have repeatedly suggested I am supposed to do—but writing this book seems a natural extension of that energy. It has taken five years to put me in front of my computer screen and type.

Humankind is driven to expand our horizons; to create, to change, to love. When you act next be aware that your very specific actions are impacting the world around you in unimagined ways. If you are going to throw a pebble in the pond, do make it count for something quite special.

16 mirror, mirror

When we respect the nude, we will no longer have any shame about it.
—Robert Henri, American painter, 1865–1929 (né Robert Henry Cozad)

. . . stepping out of her Orlon shift and underwear as blithely as though she'd undressed publicly all her life. She didn't fuss over her flesh; didn't apologize for or try to hide the pimple on her left thigh. But at each break in the five hour session she crossed the room, and still unabashedly naked, silently inspected Yuliang's progress.
—The Painter from Shanghai, Jennifer Cody Epstein, 2011

The ugliest characteristic of human beings might be our innate ability to cause emotional harm to one another. This is especially true of family members whose intimate knowledge of us allows them to 'push our buttons' with such cutting accuracy it can take the resolve of Mahatma Ghandi not to respond without a contre-riposte of equal intensity.

At 12 years of age my body had bloomed with ferocious abandon. I distinctly recall wearing a yellow and white gingham check bikini with appliqued oranges that summer. At 5'4" a 128 pounds with a 27" waist, 34c" bust and 36" hip measurements I certainly looked much more a woman in her twenties than a lowly pre-teen. If all this wasn't a bit much to deal with I was also ridiculously naïve. At a summer gathering at friends of my parents, 19 and 20 year old man/boys were playing 'catch' with me in the pool. I still recall just how fast my father appeared, told them my age and to put me down, immediately. That same year my brother poked me in the stomach and told me I was fat. Perception is a funny thing.

If this scene between siblings plays out as frequently as I believe it does can it be any wonder, when in combination with our body obsessed society, we continue to cultivate girls who abuse their bodies because they don't fit a skewed view of 'normal.' Unable to achieve their perceived level of perfection they feel worthless and binge then purge, or starve, or cut or burn themselves.

I was browsing the clearance section of an off-price retailer for a pair of sandals where nearby an absolutely b-e-a-u-t-i-f-u-l girl was trying shoes on with her mom. The mom was clearly physically smaller—either naturally or by obsessively working out. The daughter, strong, muscular, perhaps 5'10" with the most amazing face and gorgeous hair and startling, and incredibly sad to me, burn marks covering her exquisitely long legs. I wanted to burst into tears, or shake her and say "can't you see what I see?" or both. I had to walk away with my heart breaking.

Intellectually we all know that the air brushed images of magazine covers and found on the glossy pages within portray unrealistic physical perfection for both genders, and these have dulled our appreciation for authenticity. Collectively we were never intended to look like Barbie dolls or their human equivalent in the form of J.Crew© or Ralph Lauren© models. Humankind would cease to exist if coupling was only endorsed between people who were impossibly beautiful.

My dear gal pal 'Annaliese' (not her real name) is the youngest of four. In the natural order of things this means she experienced threefold what I had with my own brother calling me fat. In the Monopoly© game of our respective lives I got an unrealised "Pass Go, Collect $200" card while she picked up the tipping point card packed with an extra 30 years of tightly wound societal and cultural neurosis to be perfect—meaning thin and petite. Where my generation endured blindingly dull, but relatively benign, 'food pyramid' movies, Annaliese's was charged to keep food journals documenting everything eaten over the course of a two week period. Perhaps with her own food issues, as I witnessed at the lunch table of my niece in 1st grade, a well-meaning yet clueless teacher reviewed Annaliese's journal and told her what she was eating was wrong. She didn't treat the contents of the journal like a math formula or incorrect grammar asking what might be better choices she just outright told a 5th grader that what she was eating was wrong. To the foundation of self-doubt put in place by her siblings' teasing, her very reasonable desire to emulate a beautiful older sister and the noxious brew of hormonal changes which take place in every preteen was now this knowledge, instilled by an authority figure, that what she was eating was wrong. In totality it was much too much for an eleven-year-old to handle, it was what pushed my friend over the edge to anorexia.

Telling her family she didn't like the way this or that tasted Annaliese stopped eating. In the 6th grade, at 5'5" in height, she weighed less than 80 lbs. and found herself attending outpatient sessions three times a week at her local hospital. In high-school, better but not completely healed, she took an obsessive approach to looking at herself in the mirror. By her own admission this was to make sure that her body hadn't changed in the half hour since eating. She then began a tussle with bulimia (which she thankfully hated) to correct the perceived damage eating had done to her body. She credits the proverbial 'dangling carrot,' the ability to continue playing sports as reward, for getting healthy and saving her life. Just for a second, what if she hadn't had parents who were paying attention? A coach who held out his hand with the promise of continuing athletics if only she took care of herself and ate?

Today, she's a size 8, and healthy at about a 147 lbs. but still has trouble trying on clothes in department stores, those mirrors!, and the corrupted way that American men, her pool of dating material in their twenties, have come to view her against the impossible cultural standard of thin she will never realise. In Europe men (of all ages) fall at her feet with her Rapunzel blond locks, blue eyes, effervescent personality and true physical beauty. She is a talented college athlete in her senior year at a prestigious university graduating with a degree in history and going onto graduate school. The pain she suffered—still suffers from—is significant enough to bring her to tears as she expanded upon her story, the part I knew as well as what I had already guessed. When I suggested that I could leave her out of this chapter she was quite adamant that she wanted you, the reader, to know. To know her story so you'd be aware. To read this so you might understand how vulnerable a single word can make a child on the cusp of adolescence. So that maybe one little girl didn't buy into the whole myth of perfection and then self-loathe because she wasn't someone else's ideal. So that that little girl would know that her hair would get thinner too, and that even as her body would eventually heal her hair would not grow back in as strong and healthy as it had once been. So that she'd know that those dark circles under her eyes at 21 could have been avoided. She wanted me to tell her story so big brothers and sisters, parents, and other relatives, teachers and schoolmates could see the damage they do to others because something inside of them is insecure or that they 'want better' for the child they think they are helping. The only other thing she wanted was her name changed so it wouldn't hurt her family to know that though she's better things are still so raw for her.

I know a remarkably talented, curious, exotically striking, intellectually gifted college senior whose efforts to honour her body have been diligent and netted amazing results. She lifts weights two hours a day with a room full of men training as if for the Olympics. She's also a swimmer, physically powerful (like a lioness) and also 5'10", and for a white girl has rhythm that would make J-Lo or Beyoncé pout with envy. Her mom is itty-bitty, doesn't evidently eat (much) and with all the best intentions in the world is making her daughter miserable checking on her eating foodstuffs and if she's 'cheating.'

You know how this happens? Petite women marry physically prow men over six feet tall. When they mate and have children their coupled genetics don't necessarily produce big boys and small girls. Stop trying to make your kids over in your image! Allow me to suggest you love your kids FULLY AND COMPLETELY just as they are. Encourage them to be happy first and foremost, smart and capable secondly, bring out their unique gifts with praise, and then, just maybe, their weight (or lack) will never be an issue for them to conquer.

I was lying on my back at the end of the dock at a friend's lake house. It was suddenly overcast and threatening storm, and it was a very windy afternoon. After my workout swim in the morning and swimming on and off all afternoon with one of her daughters, I was stretching my legs (90 degree angle to my body) upwards. In truth I was also marvelling that upon inspection I do not have a single spider or varicose vein on my legs (something that my grandparents painfully suffered and under-went surgery to repair). Having watched what I was doing from the cottage my girlfriend, a recovering bulimic, then joined me and paid me a truly heartfelt compliment saying that I had the best body image of any woman she knows. Ah yes, but if you could be a fly on the wall at my parents' at any of my visits home post my divorce (in 1991) you would hear something like, "you've gained weight," or "you'll have a better chance of finding another husband if you'd go on a diet." The fact that I am comfortable in my skin has nothing to do with familial commentary, nor should it. In the end it's always just about how we come to value ourselves.

This is not to say that I am thrilled with every aspect of my body. I have cellulite. I have (old) stretch marks. At the time I am writing this book even with my daily 2 hour swims I am still likely carrying an extra 50 pounds around (I won't get on a scale). What makes me easy in my body is that it is the only one I have, most of the time it responds as I need it to in all the ways I want. It's strong and increasingly flexible (again) and I am really, very, healthy. When I ran in high school and college and only during cooler weather I was buried in my double layer varsity hoodie and sweats or my favourite cousin's gift of an Ohio State crew neck sweatshirt. In being a prissy girl I admit a concession to red tinted lip colour but this did little to offset the mud I was most often covered with, being sopping wet or dodging snow. There was nothing attractive about this look, pretty it wasn't meant to be. I was on the road to burn off stress, last nights' chicken wings, or purge the remnants of a lingering cold but it really wasn't about fitness or attractiveness.

You need only to spend 10 minutes in any locker-room to witness first-hand how obsessed we are with our body images. I watched, fascinated, as a woman got fully dressed over her towels and pulled the towel out from under her bra and t-shirt rather than be seen. While the stretch clothing clings to every curve, and the preening which takes place prior to actually working out can be astonishing, her dressing ritual was striking. I have a theory that the reflection, in the eyes of the beholder, is inaccurate—tilted more toward 'I am so fat' rather than seeing the human form in all its subtle beauty.

 137

I don't have body envy; what I have is a connoisseurs' appreciation for beauty including the human body. As we can look at Michelangelo's David and marvel at the physicality of this Renaissance era man (and perhaps wonder what he was like in bed) or the perfection of the Venus di Milo's breasts I can admire and respect the work (or natural grace) exhibiting in a toned body without wishing to look like someone who is a size two.

For my 39th birthday I packed myself off to Vienna and Budapest. There were many reasons for this journey (more on that elsewhere in this book) in blustery mid-February, but I can assure you that all were unrelated to chasing my own physical perfection. Nevertheless, a singular, unexpected moment of grace related to my body was mine to claim in the least expected place imaginable—the waters within the Hotel Gellert & Spa.

As Americans, possibly as North Americans because I do notice similar behaviour with my Canadian neighbours, we have this tragic fixation with our bodies being perfect. And being naked, especially being naked in front of other people, or a lot of other people is terrifying. Until my 39th birthday I was almost as guilty of this mind-set as any other self-conscious American, but something transformational happened to my modesty in Budapest.

At the time I was not even close to the 145 pounds of the average 5'5" American woman. My quite naked body was being slathered in healing mud by a much larger (than me) muscular Hungarian woman. Some went to my sciatica, more on both knees and especially on my right shoulder—the things that start to hurt as middle age approaches from using our bodies to play, work, and to love. Bundled in plastic wrap, then in huge cotton towels, to allow the minerals to work in conjunction with my body heat, I was ushered to a small cot to rest until whatever proscribed period of time had passed. Unwrapped and taken to a tiled shower I was subsequently rinsed off with the equivalent of a fire hose—almost too institutional to describe. Following this 'treatment' you enter the spa waters within an elaborately tiled, pillared and arched ceiling space in the Gellert's basement. 200 other women ages 14 to 90 naked and myself and one other woman, a Canadian, are the only ones seen in bathing suits. Oh! How! Embarrassing! It wasn't their nakedness which embarrassed me but for my own apparent prudery. What to do? The point isn't what I did or didn't do, there are lots of hours and lots of miles covered both metaphorically and physically between our birth and the age of 39 and no direct route from Boston to Budapest—you live but once.

Every one of these women bore her youth or age, pregnancies, surgeries (some quite brutal and without reconstruction), scars, stretch marks, cellulite, just plain fat and especially her breasts in various shapes and levels of perkiness with a natural grace and ease that would be unimaginable in the States. I was suitably impressed. After the waters are 'taken' then it's off to the eucalyptus oil massage—still quite naked and no choice for it—a smaller than average hand towel barely covered my backside—to receive a pummelling to my muscles which resulted in bruises I sported for weeks. I am sure it was 'good for me.'

Years later I am struck by how in the locker-room of my health club even the most physically beautiful are swathed in multiple towels and contort to dress themselves beneath these rather than as the old expression goes 'let it all hang out.' Why are we, in Western society, all so neurotic about our bodies? I love the idea of Enrique Iglesias song *Don't Turn Off The Lights*© spurring on a mini-revolution of people everywhere suddenly becoming so comfortable in their own skin that being naked in front of a lover engaged in the most pleasurable of human activities is so not a big deal. Of course there are limits imposed in good taste and appropriateness, as well as cultural norms.

 139

I recall my brother sharing the some of the details a trip taken in his twenties. He woke up a little the worse the wear from the night before, stumbled to the beach in whatever Mediterranean town he was in and sobered in short order at the sight of topless women, long past their prime, sunbathing and swimming. When I was much younger and every physical asset was as high and tight as it could possibly be, I admit to topless sunbathing 3,000 miles from home (where no one was going to know me) in an isolated cove La Jolla, California. The validation of having men simply admire the beauty of your body in passing overhead at the rim of the cove and give you a 'thumbs up' is very cool. No wolf calls, no attempts at groping, just an appreciation for the physical form which happened to be me at that one tiny moment in time is not forgotten.

I can't say that women are irrationally hard on themselves, men exhibit this neurosis too—though perhaps to lesser degree because they are so ingrained to be omnipotent that it 'must' transcend to their physicality. Thankfully many have gotten over the hair loss thing and just shave their heads.

Joe is a highly accomplished salesman—not the way you might think, I am talking about selling enterprise technology solutions into Fortune 100 companies. BIG money. He gives off the same kind of magnetism that a predatory animal about to run its quarry to ground does. He decided, at age 44, to get back into competitive wrestling (in his youth 20+ years earlier he was ranked #5 in the United States just shy of making the Olympic team). He trained as relentlessly as he sold, honing his body and his mental advantage simultaneously. Finally ready to compete he headed off to a nationally sanctioned beach wrestling tournament to compete in the Masters division—except no one his age showed up. So the organizers decide to put him in the senior division with men half his age, Navy Seals and Special Ops guys, likely figuring they'd earn great PR no matter what. The old expression about age and treachery beating youth and skill bears fruit. Not once but twice Joe dominates his half-age rivals to take the national title. He's obviously quite fit. As I was sitting when we met I honestly hadn't noticed his height. In truth, I still hadn't noticed even as he walked me to his car to drive me home. With all of his accomplishments, with an enviable physique at 50, Joe was hung up on two things: his 5'7" height—which he mentioned at least three times once we got up from the table—and losing his edge. He said that he, and any other man, was only as valuable as his last deal, his wealth or his ability to lead a company, because when these things slipped a man retired, not because they want to but because he said they are no longer relevant. The primal need to conquer and validate superiority didn't diminish with a man's age as long as a man had his 'edge' (in whatever form that might be) he was still going to be attractive to a large percentage of women. Just as young men are anxious to get in the game, loose their virginity, conquer the world, men who are old enough to have become secure in their value as people are still seemingly hung up on their physical presence and attracting mates.

None of this actually occurred to me. All I know is that every man develops his own unique appeal (to me) based largely upon his intellect, humour and confidence. In Joe's case he piqued my sexual curiosity just as much as my gorgeous shoe repair guy who I have known for 30 years!

Our nerve endings do not discriminate nor are they capable of distinguishing varying degrees of attractiveness. They aren't able to gauge how flawlessly perfect our outward appearance may or may not be, their only purpose is to convey the tactile pleasure we derive from touching someone we love. Nerves exist to keep us safe from physical pain (fire, acid spills, cuts, bruises, broken bones) by creating a memory of the lesser harms found in our childhoods or to pull back from, flee in fact, from danger that goes back to our evolutionary origins. But it's the pleasure each nerve ending can provide through our fingertips traveling across the expanse of skin in the form of giving or receiving a hug, a kiss or a caress (or more) which is to be deliciously experienced and never to be taken for granted.

I understand the result of exercise releasing endorphins and dopamine into my system to make me happy and how good it feels to work my muscles in the pool, on my bike or in the garden. But from the perspective of attracting mates I don't understand the supreme effort so many people of both genders put into maintaining or establishing prime physical presence. That somehow finding balance for our bodies needs to be met with positive self-awareness.

I am totally confused as much by extreme fitness as the self-loathing which allows cutting, burning, anorexia or bulimia to even manifest. As a casual observer I can't see the emotional pain that manifests itself in either extreme being applied to your physical being. I see you just as handsome or lovely, capable, smart, strong, or perfectly normally 'boring' looking as the rest of us. Truly, someday soon, I hope you see what I see before me.

17 the yoga sprinter

It's the 19th of July. I am post two-hour swim, post de-chlorinating . . . , finished with a second 'coldest water setting possible' shower and am in the locker room dressing. I am in a state of grace and gratitude. I have been pushing myself physically and accomplishing things previously unimaginable to my 50 year old body only a few months ago—like swimming 50 yards freestyle in 51 seconds without a flip turn! I am zoning out thinking about my swim and what I can do better tomorrow morning at 6:30.

When, suddenly.

This size 2, totally ripped, woman about my age races in, drops her bag, opens a locker, strips and redresses in a matter of seconds, I see the yoga mat and the obligatory body hugging clothes. Her frenetic rush is displacing my serene state and my ritual of slathering on sea mineral based body lotion. Her efforts to speed through the locker room are similar to a Triathlete leaving the water for their bike. I couldn't help myself, I comment, "Your energy strikes me as counter-intuitive to the purpose of yoga"—a meditative practice to connect with the Divine. She laughs and agrees, and she slips off to her next class. Next day, repeat.

Four days in a row the same interaction and then finally we really talk. She tells me her story—in greater detail than most people ever would consider with a complete stranger. I tell her that I have always believed we make some random connection with people to share information and we never know which individual is going to wind up being the teacher. I suggest, to that point, she pick up James Redfield's *The Celestine Prophecy*© and that more than anything else she learn to let things get a little out of focus so she can see everything more clearly. She doesn't look at me like I am nuts.

As part of this dialog is about her marriage I share my beliefs, especially poignant when there are kids involved. I qualify, this is NOT advice. No matter how self-absorbed the parents, how good they think they are at concealing the fighting, tension, ugliness—kids know, and they think it's their fault. This living tutorial of what marriage and family is sets the standard for a child's future choices. Just as the abused are likely to become abusers, or the damaged rearing children who struggle with self-esteem and validation, when in any marriage, right or wrong, your kids will seek out a partner which replicates the 'normal' environment you and your spouse create for them to experience.

Regardless of their age, 4, 6 or 10 or 18, discerning that any other option for a marriage exists than the example you and your spouse are providing isn't realistic. Is your marriage tender, loving, respectful, a true partnership? Or is it filled with degrading anger, sarcasm, addiction (alcohol, drugs, sex, gambling, eating or not), abuse (physical, emotional or isolating control), or the ultimate insult ambivalence? If you don't really, and truly, love yourself, loving another person is just about impossible. All the aforementioned illnesses need professional intervention and treatment. No matter how much you truly believe in and love your partner you can't fix this person. They need to fix themselves. Stay and you enable. What you earn by staying and not getting help is not martyrdom (for being such a saint and putting up with it all), what you get is a proportional level of illness of your own.

Every adult has two choices about his or her relationship. The first is to fix it no matter what it takes and the other is to find the will to get out, and commence rebuilding a life grounded in self-respect which, hopefully, also leads to finding a loving relationship that helps your kids reset their perspectives.

We exchange business cards, later I pop her off a reminder about Redfield's book.

On Jul 23, 2011, at 5:27 PM, "Teresa Fritschi" wrote:
Hi Linda,

I can't thank you enough for opening up and baring your soul this morning. Maybe it's just easier to tell a stranger but perhaps our lives have connected long ago. In any case welcome to my present life—stay as long as you want and know I am not about binding friends up to 'keep them.' Everything is cyclical and our crossing paths might also be so!

Now, go find a used book store, preferably with a New Age bent, and pick up James Redfield's The Celestine Prophecy. It's an easy read which will likely make you search even harder for answers but, if you listen with your heart instead of your head you will come to understand it's all inside us if we just slow down, calm down and let things get a little out of focus.

I am in the pool at 7 AM (when the club opens in the morning) come take the lane next to me or let's just chat at 9:30 before you head back to Penn.
Hugs,
T.

She sends me the following in response:

Hi Terry!
    Is was so great meeting u. I think nothing is an accident. I will get that book. I is interesting how u are talking about listening to my heart instead of my head. I just read an article by Martha Beck in that exact thing. Your heart is usually right:) it's how u feel when u imagine your life. When I imagine my life the way I want it to be, my heart sings, I smile and can't contain my energy:)
see u in the morning. . .

Linda:)

To which, 22 minutes later (according to the time stamp on my outgoing email), I sent her the initial draft of the proposed foreword to **All That I Need**. And she responded with:

Omg!! I love this!! I just want more as I read it!!! Do u know under the Tuscan sun is my favorite movie and I want her life. My soul sings and I get goose bumps thinking of a life like that.

Get busy, grease up the fountain pen:):) can't wait to read it when it is complete!!!!!!!
I will be there at 7. Will probably stay in the cardio and weight room. I will wander out to the pool. If i happen to miss u out there, I'll Have my phone with me. Look for me.

Glad I Met u!!

Linda, visiting her sister and taking full advantage of her sister's membership in my club, is the reason that I finally stopped ignoring my 'Diana' girlfriends,' and acquaintances alike, repetitive and impassioned suggestions that I write a book. Though I actually only use a real fountain pen for writing longhand, I picked up my figurative fountain pen and started typing. For the life of me I can't figure out—why now?

I felt my encounter with Linda warranted a transparency to potential readers, so before she left I asked her to consider contributing her parallel perspective on our meeting and conversation. The challenges she seemed struggling to find the strength to meet were hinted at in the next communication from Linda, which arrived two days later.

On 7/25/2011 12:15 PM, Linda wrote:

Hi Terry!!
Quick note, got a call from a friend yesterday and decided to hop on their pontoon boat at canadaigua lake and anchor and jump off the boat (in our clothes) and float!!
Kids loved, loved it and it was the medicine I needed!!! I know where I want to be and what i want to do now!!
Will read your excerpt as soon as I get home. I am on the side of the road rt. Now.
Had to tell u this!!
Linda

Date: Mon, 25 Jul 2011 12:48:29 -0400
I AM SO GLAD FOR THIS UPDATE - got chills.
God Bless.
Love,
t

The next day another missive, this response from Linda after receiving the draft Yoga Sprinter chapter:

Wow!! I was wondering who that size 2 was in the ripped body, seriously!! Maybe that shows how disconnected I really am..... I am reading your words like I am in the desert finding droplets of water along the way and longing for more. Wanting to come to a big basin, jump in and drink up! I picture myself floating on my back with a straw sucking up every drop of water in there. I have been emotionally dehydrated for way too long. I have committed to changing my life. I know meeting you was no accident. You are a blessing to me and as soon as this book is written, it will reach so many more....... Go for it!!!!! You have this amazing gift!! This just flows out of you... naturally....

Linda

I just read this part about marriage, kids, loving yourself. I am so speechless, touched, emotional and relieved all rolled up into one. It all comes back to loving yourself first. I have always sought out love. I have more to say—need to "sprint off" :):)

On Fri, Aug 5, 2011 at 8:12 PM, Teresa Fritschi wrote:
Dearest Yoga Sprinter,

I know that the components of life can seem too weighty a burden. Hauling us into an abyss where internal bearings are distorted and the GPS doesn't work. You MUST believe in your ability to come through this—for everyone's sake.

You are like every other parent. Too stressed, pulled in too many directions, struggling to breathe and make sure everyone, including you, is alright. You aren't alone, honest.

Even if you aren't a parent—in this economy we are all scared and overwhelmed. Ask for grace but know you deserve it.

Sometimes our greatest challenges are laid at our doorsteps so we can pull ourselves out and find the light within.

Linda, when dashing off to yoga, to sweat, try to get passed the physical and touch the emotional/mental essence of this ancient practice.

With loving kindness.
Terri

Sent: Aug 5, 2011 5:46 PM
Hi Terri,

Quick note—have not forgotten to write my half, just busy. Life has gotten Crazy again. I am trying to find a peace within me to get through it all. I try to be a good mom, i am failing at the moment. There is always tomorrow.

Sometimes choices have to be made in life to save your own. I am making those choices for the health, wellbeing and happiness if my childrwn and me. Will write more.

Gotta sweat it out in heated yoga:).) my meditation:):)
Linda

And later that day:

Hi Terri,

My GPS has been broken for years:) Bits of wisdom(from my father who died when I was 20 and my grandmother who died 5 yrs. ago) keep entering my mind at the precise moment my life needs that amazing love and guidance. They were the two people in my life who celebrated life and "tried" to teach me to live in the moment. I wondered when my life would count after being told where we were moving and what we could buy, etc. in my married life. I have begun to realize that I have been the barrier to feeling like my life counts, not anyone else. I gave everyone else the power. How foolish. I am the fool (or was:)). When you know better, you do better I once heard. Now I know better and i am fighting to do better with every breathe, every step, every word and everyday. We are much harder on ourselves than on others sadly. I have had many greatest challenges laid at my doorstep lately (love how you put that) I am taking one at a time, step by step. My grandmother would say, "you can walk,talk,see and hear, what are you complaining about." My grandma Rose was the wisest of all. She taught me much. I sat with her as she died, holding her hand telling her how much I loved her. I never had the opportunity with my father. I was too stubborn, and afraid of love, afraid to be loved. Hmmm....

Taking the yoga challenge this week. 5 days of heated yoga..Not as meditative and cleansing as Midtown yoga but it will serve it's purpose. Only get what you put into it......:):) Hope you are enjoying your weekend..

Linda

On Aug 21, 2011, at 4:23 PM, "Teresa Fritschi" wrote:

Although I KNOW that the universe set up circumstances to open both of us up, had it not been for our meeting this book would very likely never been written Linda. I am at 69 pages (not a bad bit of writing for four weeks) and feel confident of final manuscript being ready by Columbus Day weekend.
Thank you! Hope all is well.
Terri

Date: Sun, 21 Aug 2011 16:30:06 -0400:
Hi!!
With your help, i am finding myself again!! Everyone is telling me i am more animated, happy and free spirited!! My life is starting to come together!! Meeting you was no accident:) your encouragement, understanding and support came at precisely the right time in my life. Like Glenda, the good witch said "you always had it my dear" or something like that. Everyone has it within them it just has to b the rt. Time to accept it take responsibility for it. Hope to see u in the next coming weeks. I may b up this weekend and for sure labor day weekend..
With graditude,
Linda

Date: Tue, 13 Sep 2011 08:51:51 -0400
Hi Terri,
Sorry I missed your phone calls. I hope to see you soon. Trying to get back up there. Life is tough at the moment.
Linda

On Tue, Sep 13, 2011 at 8:56 AM
I want you to focus on the good stuff Linda. Hug the kids tightly when they get home
from school today. Do something unexpected with them to recapture the joy of floating on Canadaigua. Sending you happy thoughts.
T

Date: Tue, 13 Sep 2011 09:01:33 -0400
My husband wants to divorce me. He is just waiting for me to 'get on my feet.' I don't
have a job and am currently looking into my options. Life is scary now.
Linda

This announcement of his desire to divorce is obviously shocking and hurtful to her. I
know she's been trying to bring joy back to the marriage. They've been to counselling and
he doesn't (according to her) bother to respond in their sessions. I admit, based upon what
little I know, my perception of his role in their marriage is one of indifference or a resigna-
tion to live with the status quo.

We all know that the scope of every relationship is different. Every marriage from
lasting from two to fifty years has seen 'its fair share.' The state of the global economy is
applying untold levels of stress to everyone, more still for parents. There are two sides to
every story, some less balanced than others. People get restless, or bored. For a marriage to
flourish and grow and especially last, both individuals need to be fully vested in it, doing
nice because they want to rather than because it is expected of them. I read once, somewhere, that the person who cares the least is the one who actually controls a relationship.
Ambivalence is a terrible thing in general but a death knell in a relationship. People fall out

of love for all kinds of reasons but largely, I think, because their partner somehow ceases to be the viable, interesting individual that they married or one becomes a much more interesting person than the other leaving them living in past that isn't sustainable. Most importantly, at some point (some) couples cease being lovers and become mini-corporations taking on the various tasks necessary to run their family. The magic that made them a couple disappears as the 'honey do' lists and the responsibilities of aging parents clash with (hopefully) raising well adjusted, charming, healthy, intelligent, productive children. While they are trying to accomplish the most important job on the planet, they stop saying please, or thank you, and meaning it. They stop doing the thousand little kindnesses that they freely devoted energy to when they were dating or first married. They assume that their spouse will take care of (fill in the blank) at the same time they take that individual for granted for running the family unit. To survive, to function, partners take a stance of either 'choosing their battles,' suffering in silence, retorts of sarcasm, or escapism (solo trips to the spa for message and masks, fishing or hunting or special events or, affairs with their greater degree of self-indulgence). Am I the only one that sees that this is counter to the whole process of raising children?

I don't have any solutions to offer other than training yourself to tackle the contents of your lists with a level of happiness. That said you do not have to do a Happy Dance each time you tick something off the list. It's kind of like the practise of smiling while on the phone while trying to resolve something unpleasant—the shape of our faces shifts our vocal patterns to sound less angry or antagonistic. As a result the perception of the listener becomes more responsive because they don't feel threatened or maligned. This proposed shift in attitude as a couple, as a parent or caretaker for a parent applies equally for a single person is to take joy in tiny bits so that cumulatively Life is good® really comes to mean something.

Date: Tue, 13 Sep 2011 13:20:30 +0000
If he wants the divorce then he gets to pay for the privilege. You need to be able to take care of the kids and you, and he has obligations. You need to talk to a VERY good divorce attorney and because he wants the divorce he gets to pay for that too! Be a strong POWERFUL woman that I know you are and not a door mat—pick up the phone and find a lawyer right now!

And then, silence. We are barely acquainted but I am concerned. I can't do anything but keep Linda in my prayers and hope for some version of the best for her and her family.

Sun, 18 Sep 2011 20:53:09 -0400
Hey There!
I am bring the kids up to my sister's Sept. 29 – Oct. 2nd. Hope to see you at Midtown or maybe we can get together somehow. Would love to see you !! If you see Michele at Midtown, tell her we are coming!!!

On 10/2/2011 11:27 AM, Linda wrote:

Hi Teresa!!
You were no where to be found at Midtown this weekend. Are you ok? Did you move??? I will be back up in two weeks and I am doing the Yoga Teacher Training there, so I will be up often. I have decided to enroll in the Institute for Integrative

Nutrition and become a wellness coach!!! I am beyond excited for my new life. Can't wait to see where it takes me...
I hope you are doing well and we get to catch up in a few weeks.

Linda :)

Sat, 08 Oct 2011 13:34:46 -0400
Sorry Linda,
I am more than okay and can't wait to see you! If you have time your portion of the book should be in my hands this week as I am nearly done!!! On schedule, Columbus Day weekend was when I wanted to finish and I am at 240 pages!

 155

Sending you much happiness for your new career path!
Hugs,
t

Date: Sat, 8 Oct 2011 13:44:58 -0400
We will b up next weekend and i will b up 8 weekends between oct. 28-feb. For yoga teacher training:)) i am
Overjoyed and my revelations lately in my life. I believe every
thing happens for a reason. Thank u for being a part of my life:)

Linda

Date: Sat, 08 Oct 2011 13:47:56 -0400
I am in HAPPY TEARS for you Linda. See you next weekend.

Sun, 9 Oct 2011 21:30:04 -0400
Hi Teresa!!

So many people have come into my life this year as if my father (who died when I was 20) sent each and every one of you. I have had many conversations with him since his death asking him to help me "figure out" my life. As if each one of you were "staged" this year to present yourselves to me in such an orchestrated way. What really impacted me was when you (Teresa) spoke to me in the Midtown locker room as I was coming in from a calming yoga class commenting on my 'yoga sprinting.' I found it hysterically funny and connected with you immediately. I then 'sprinted' out to the weight room:) The conversations we had after that really made me think about my life and how that one instance in the locker room really reflected my life. I have been "yoga sprinting" my way thinking I was finding my "chi" and also successfully raising 3 children at the same time and dealing with a failing marriage. Ha,ha... who was I fooling?

I read part of Steve Jobs' commencement speech. The part that captures me is: " Have the courage to follow your heart and intuition. They somehow already know what you truly want to become. Everything else is secondary."—Steve Jobs. I spent the first half of my life fighting my heart, not wanting to be like my father thinking he wasn't "successful" enough and I never wanted to end up like that. The opposite was really true. He was successful at the most important lesson in life which is follow your heart and intuition and everything else is secondary.

That day in the locker room was pivotal for me. That was the launching pad for changing my life from feeling desperate and depressed to knowing I will survive this, flourish and be stronger because of it.

Date: Mon, 10 Oct 2011 11:45:52 +0000

Oh Linda, what a wonderful way to start my morning! If you believe, as I do, that we're all energy (which never dies) and is connected to all other beings and their energy then it's entirely rational and reasonable that your Dad has been guiding you 'home.' Success is absolutely about loving well, finding pleasure in the mundane, cherishing the 'sweet-spots' in the moment and calling them back to you 'as needed.'

Yesterday mid-morning I was swimming but I had to stop and experience the joy as one of summer's last bright ambassadors, a Monarch butterfly flitted around the pool deck near my lane resting and eating. Then it rose over my head and danced on air currents above the pool for five minutes and was gone. Was it more productive to sink back into the water for more laps or watch the butterfly? We both know the answer. Have a wonderful day! See you soon!

Terri

Date: Sun, 23 Oct 2011 19:08:22 -0400
I love you!!! You are such an inspiration to me. I know our meeting was not chance, it was meant to be. You are a beautiful person Teresa!! Connected forever:)
I would love to be there to celebrate the launch of your book. Will see if I can arrange it (kids,bus,school,etc.)

See you next weekend I hope!!
p.s. Just a few days ago, I told my husband "you forced me to take a look at my life and change it—thank you" Without all the pain, there is no pleasure....... You need

to really feel defeat to appreciate winning.. I feel like I am giving myself some grace and forgiving and it feels amazing. No one can just tell you to forgive, you have to be ready,willing and able to. Whatever happens to me, I know I'll be alright, finally!!!

I am so proud of you for undertaking such a big task. A book is monumental!! Congrats, congrats, congrats!!!!!!!!
Linda:)

Do I know what is going to happen with Linda and her kids? Nope, and neither does she. She'll complete her training as a yoga instructor at my health club, just as I learned to ski to get through my divorce, and then I hope the world will open up for her allowing for personal satisfaction and discovery and stability that she's hungered for and that her kids so richly deserve. Her first major step of expressing forgiveness and gratitude toward her husband was as much about taking personal responsibility for her life going forward as releasing any lingering (negative) resentment and regret.

We meet people when we need to know something, believe more in ourselves, take on a challenge we've put off too long because life simply gets in the way. She was my catalyst, I doubt I was hers but if meeting me truly became the lynch pin to get her moving I can only take credit for being a messenger she needed at that particular moment. If you haven't seen Andie MacDowell, William Hurt and Bob Hoskins in the 1996 film *Michael*© with John Travolta in the leading role, he plays as an angel come to Earth—make a quick stop to Netflix© and rent it to further understand what I mean about messengers and timing being everything.

18 knowing love

Love is the only just and holy war. Two friends pledge loyal opposition to one another. I vow I will defend the integrity of my separate being and respect the integrity of your being. We will meet only as equals; I will present myself in fullness of being and will expect the same of you. I will not cower, apologize or condescend. Our covenant will be to love one another justly and powerfully; to establish inviolable boundaries; to respect our separate sanctuaries. We will remain joined in the sweet agony of dialogue, the contest of conversation, the dialectic of love until we arrive at synthesis.
—Fire in the Belly: On Being A Man,© Sam Keen, 1992

Is there anyone in the English speaking world who still hasn't seen *Love Actually?*© In truth I hadn't thought of this charming movie until the Knowing Love chapter was fully complete. I was re-reading and editing, a thankless, boring job requiring suitable music to be in the right frame of mind—what could be a better choice than the soundtrack to a movie exclusively about love? The story line spans every variation of love culminating on

Christmas—when, of course, we are supposedly loving more powerfully and perfectly than any other time of year. That movie captures the exhilaration of an elementary school crush, betrayal within what appeared to be a 'perfectly normal marriage' of some years, the aching love only a widower (or widow) can carry around, the discomfort of love under one's nose that makes us deny, cast aside, and runaway from, only to (hopefully) figure it out in time to make a go of it, the discovery of love between best friends and the love of a sibling to the point of extreme sacrifice. My life, and yours, is rich with examples of all of these and more. I shared the final excerpted version with friends in conjunction with my submission to a shelter publication for its annual Life Lessons Essay Contest. And suddenly I had yet another example of love which nourishes our being—priceless, very dear friends.

From: Chris Lopez
Date: Tue, 13 Sep 2011 16:18:50 -0400
T—we are in the basque region. I just read your life lessons to Chris aloud over wine and the last bit of our most amazing dinner...we love you, you are incredible!
Love,
Mr and Mrs Lopez

From: Teresa Fritschi
Sent: Tuesday, September 13, 2011 04:38 PM
OMG I can't BELIEVE you two would take time out of your honeymoon to honour me with your time and love! Eat a Gypsy's Arm for me!

It's been long said that there are three courses of love to be experienced across the span of our lives. In youth love is linked to passion, in adulthood material surety and in maturity love is about companionship. I think then, if we are fortunate enough to thoroughly enjoy the first, and are confident enough in our own capabilities to not 'need' the second, that the third should be our reward.

To enjoy laughter and convivial delight, to relish in another's intellect and defined charm without desire to alter, to celebrate professional and personal success with a partner equal in merit and tastes and to continually find attraction in their countenance is a truer blessing than any other. I can't speak to why some marriages thrive in friendship—but suspect that respect and love for oneself contributes mightily.

Remember those Pepto-Bismol® pink desk sets with the blue metal legs found in elementary schools in the sixties? I was in the 2nd grade and a boy named Paul put pink rose buds in the holes of my overturned chair for two weeks until Mrs Gumm put a stop to 'the nonsense.'

There was a man, married nearly 40 years, who lived in my apartment building for a single year. This trial 'non-divorcing separation' was simply so he could breathe. As he retired he realised just how empty his wife's life had become—living exclusively for him, his interests, for time to spend with him, doing absolutely nothing for herself. His wife had never developed her own personality beyond who she was at the time of their marriage. If he played golf with friends she waited at home alone. If he went to a coffee shop to read she'd wait for his return. He took the simplest pleasure from making a pot of coffee his studio. He'd come back from walking in our rather arts-y and architecturally significant neighbourhood alone like he'd won the Irish Sweepstakes—on top of the world. He didn't date anyone except his wife during this period. At the end of the year he moved back into their home with sadness at both the prospect and losing this tiny renewed piece of his being. It nearly broke my heart.

The whirl of activity surrounding senior year of high school, yet, my 'adopted' twin nieces (the daughters of one of my dearest friends) Kate and Julia, along with their remaining cousin at home Megan, still make time to visit their grandfather at his extended-care facility. Joe sometimes plays Bingo or Scrabble,® often watches a Yankees© game, and frequently falls asleep. But they go, willingly, to visit a couple of times each week.

How do you know that it's love? It doesn't need to scream at you, or shouldn't. It should 'feel' like a thick oversized cashmere sweater—soft, warm, comforting, and most of all, reliable.

History's greatest lovers have been ill-fated. Had they overcome circumstance, scheming relatives, scorned lovers, political intrigue, if the Moirae, the three furies, had shown greater favour would we even know the names of Tristan and Isolde, Abelard and Héloïse, Mark Anthony and Cleopatra, Paris and Helen today?

Walk in Boston Common, Manhattan's Central Park, along the narrow sidewalks of San Francisco's Chinatown and you'll see them still holding hands or her arm threaded through his as they walk, often with canes, still glowing, chattering away like tiny birds or not at all, enviable in companionable silence, these lovers in their eighties and nineties both a sort of shade of griege touched with sea foam reflecting a translucent pink unique to age. "Hold onto him darling, a good man is hard to find!" They smile. Announce they've been married for some astonishing number of decades and he says, clearly still smitten as a school boy, "she is the only girl I have ever loved."

The knowledge of love is almost cellular isn't it? An intimate springing forth which can't be contained. We look in his/her eyes and the world spins, our heart clenches and unfolds in wonder and willingness to explore all life has to offer. If we're really lucky we mate, as swans do, for life and it's long and deliriously happy—even when it's as boring as watching paint dry. My great uncle Eddie and his bride Wanda were like that. Married in 1928, together for nearly 75 years—he passing at 96, she within six months at 93. They exuded kindness and ease, provided a framework of unconditional love for one another, their daughters and their families, and all who knew them. I can still hear her say, "Now Eddie", taste her cheesecake, smell his greenish tinted cigars, see them pull up in the near ancient AMC Rambler,© feel the presence of their love though they have been dead since 2002.

You stand in the doorway to a clap board church or a grand cathedral. Behind you there's a breath of autumn rain, damp leaf smells, pockets of brittle blue against shades of dove greys colouring the sky. In front of you, though there are many, only one human being—the one you are about to marry. When did this happen? How to come to know so exquisitely that this man more than any other, is who you could love as justly and powerfully as the Divine ordained?

The weekend following New York State's historic adoption of legislation granting gay couples the right to legally wed I was out riding my bike. Posing for photos in front of The Unitarian Church were two gorgeous women who had just been joined in marriage, the brides with joyful smiles with their exquisite bridal party all dressed in a dark sage green silk. The local Gay Pride Parade breaking up around them. I focus on the sunshine radiating warmth, dappled through the trees and not the Evangelical Christians who clearly are not promoting God's love through their bull-horn rantings and call out "Well done ladies! Congratulations." Honestly I don't care who you love as long as you love and do so completely.

How could anyone deny love has many forms? My most profound knowledge of love came in unique episodes transcending time.

Hideo, as I have introduced previously, is a much revered healer and Shinto priest of 85 years young. He has this amazing ability to be in 'contact' at a precisely required time. On the occasion of our meeting he indicated we had known each other in a previous lifetime—he being my brother and teaching me all about love I only discovered three years later. Hideo, I am quite certain I have forgotten a good portion of the lessons you imparted. I pray I get this right.

Secondly, inadvertently the man who is responsible for my meeting Hideo is Richard.

Though I don't share his memory, I have no doubt of his 'cognitive recollection' of an event taking place some 900 years prior to our current time in what is now likely France. Richard says he is standing in chain mail, broad sword in hand at the back of a small stone church. He maintains that I, in 'this' former life, am kneeling on a prie-dieu wearing a thick gray velvet gown praying. He clearly believes me to be some level of aristocracy but something more as well. He takes his sword and drives it into the stones pledging, essentially, to always have my back. Richard was the best friend of Hideo's friend Blane's sister before she died of cancer. Blane maintains that Richard has been chasing my soul around the universe for the last 900 years and has yet to learn lessons and perhaps repent for some 'very bad' wrongs committed so long ago and thus the reason why I remain 'out of his reach.'

Let's assume both of these memories are real. Does that mean our souls burden our karmic drama until we 'get it right'? Why, for some, finding love remains elusive, and why others are called to a higher love to be monks and nuns to offer themselves as vessels for Divine love of mankind? Does love, in all its permutations, possess a physical manifestation in the form of energy which also never dies? Is love, like a star burning out, capable of sustaining its brilliance for a couple billion years?

Love cannot grow, flourish, sustain, nurture, set an example or comfort anyone else unless it exists within each of us as individuals. Self-esteem, the greatest form of human love, is the guarantor of the capacity to love others. We can rise from ashes like the mythical phoenix with the presence of love. When we give it away, quietly and without need for adoration or acclaim, love multiples exponentially like spring bulbs, like cascading waters down the face of a mountain, like the visual confection presented as a flock of pink flamingos takes off in flight. It is beauty in every form imaginable. It can make us gasp with delight or to catch our breath because we are gloriously overwhelmed. For most of us love will never be sweeping poetry delirious with adjectives—it's much more likely to be formed with crayons, coloured pencils and water soluble paint on a horizontal piece of 8 ½ x 11 paper attached to the refrigerator.

There's the physical love shared with longing and passion, tenderness and innate understanding which can result in perfectly synchronised, simultaneous climax. Once experienced makes you willing to go without—if even reluctantly—forever.

Love isn't either chocolate or vanilla—unless it's homemade tapioca pudding, Crème brûlée, warm chocolate chip cookies with a glass of cold milk as you get home from school or molten chocolate cake oozing Belgian decadence across your tongue. I know for certain that love is strawberry flavoured in the form of my Aunt Jeanne's Jell-O™ salad with crushed pecans, pineapple, strawberries, bananas and a thick layer of sour cream, although maybe it can be updated with plain Greek yogurt!

The colour of love isn't the deep throbbing of Valentine red but rather like the spectrum of light in reverse, pure white with the slightest tint of blue-y lavender. The full range of colour, of life, brought together in one perfect calming shade.

There's the kind of love a parent has for a child . . . dragging hoses out of the basement at 11PM to flood the frozen woods glazing the ice to near mirror perfection, providing recipes to hotel chefs far away from home to ensure a grown daughter has her special birthday cake as she turns 29, sitting in the pouring rain for athletic activities and driving hundreds of miles to look at college campuses.

Dig a hole, work compost and topsoil together, plant a tree on the day you fall in love with the sound and smell of your baby's first breath and a second one 12 feet apart on their first birthday. Twenty years later watch from the kitchen window as they lay in a hammock strung between the two trees which have marked their life, their arms around their first lover reading to them, the world slipping away on a Sunday afternoon. Your fiancé 'almost' manages to keep himself and his glass of wine within the boundaries of a different hammock, alas the hammock wins and he lands on the ground next to the farm pond. Hilarity reigns.

Listen to and feel the rise of the body of your dog against yours to know what love is.

Imagine standing in an ancient stone gateway, where hundreds of thousands of people have trod before you. The common and the extraordinary united in the human genome all passing the same way. Inherently you know there is an unseen energy to tap into—and when you do, the person you become walking through this portal is different, more complete. When you reach the ability to consistently live in the moment—consciously embracing the pursuit of pleasure and beauty, of fulfilment and challenging yourself to stretch the boundaries prescribed by society (or yourself) you will always find yourself pleasantly surprised by the outcome. It's the same in loving—yourself first, and in time, the partner whose commitment to also present his/herself 'in fullness of being' isn't forced but simply as natural as taking a breath.

Listen to your inner voice, that intuition that can almost guarantee that you are not about to make a stupid choice. Have the conviction to follow through as Ewan McGregor's' character Christian does in *Moulin Rouge*© singing *Come What May*,© live your life with intention, powerfully. It isn't so different from simply getting through each day—it just has the exquisite possibilities of living without regret. The principles applied to unleashing your 4 year-old self to the joy of splashing through a 5" deep rain puddle is the same for falling in love with someone—it's about letting go. Find the ability to feel the exquisiteness of a single moment and believe me you will know what is possible when it comes to loving.

My dearest, nearly longest friendship is with a woman 26 years my senior. I love Doris as much for the synergy of our understanding of art and antiques, though vastly different tastes, mutual interests in gardening and cooking, as for her tender hearts' filled encouragement over the years. She has been more 'family' to me than I could adequately explain. But it was her marriage to Bob that was so very extraordinary. Although I never heard a complaint against him, I am sure there must have been at least one. She had her interests, he had his own and then they had this beauty of shared space that gave each exactly what they needed to thrive.

Bob was largely absent from a presence within our friendship until the last six years of his life but in those years he fully adopted me. When I came to visit them in their suburban Buffalo, NY, home Bob would join us at the kitchen table for 'catching up.' He read the draft texts of pages for my website praising the effort and expressing "I can tell how much research you've put into this." He was mechanically gifted. He might have thought I was a 'little off' with the passion expressed for my car but he commented more than once what a great looking car Duncan was and always enquired about if he was running alright. I would be hard pressed to love him anymore on a personal level but it was because he so clearly unconditionally loved my girlfriend, though not to a point of idolatry, that I loved

Bob most. To be in the presence of such a love affair is an honour. It gives us all hope to know that differences in culture, social station, and geographic heritage can be overcome and that such a magical can exist.

Remember the Sandra Bullock/John Cusack movie *Serendipity*© or Ms Bullock opposite Keanu Reeves in *The Lake House*© with its lovely reference to Jane Austen's *Persuasion*? The ever perfect happy ending presented as Mr Darcy and Elizabeth Barrett overcome all in Ms Austen's *Pride and Prejudice*? Even if some measure of palpable pain is on the menu, the promise of consummation outweighs the potential of immolation. Despite being examples of feel good fiction, our real lives can also have astonishing examples of timing being everything and love conquering all.

In my life there have been hundreds of kisses shared with boys in 7th grade to men in their sixties. But it's always the first one that determines the erotic dimension between potential lovers.

The late November wind and rain slash away as I stand in a doorway on the Isle of Skye. I am returning, ounce for ounce, the passionate kisses of a man I have known less than 48 hours. A man whose innate knowledge of my being (or whose 'cheek' as the Brits say) five hours earlier laid claim to me with a gesture of such startling intimacy as to totally undo me, a woman 13 years his senior. The seemingly innocent gesture was a 'nothing' in and of itself—simply brushing a wet curl off my face—but he did this in front of a roomful of strangers, making me feel more exposed and vulnerable than any other time in my life before or since. Rational thought, such as sensibly coming in out of the rain, escapes us both. The raw weather stokes every gasping breath for more of this moment.

Odd, all these years later, I can honestly say it's the closest I have ever come to feeling exactly like a romance novel heroine. The only thing missing from this scene is the kilt this man would be wearing the next day.

I believe in 15 seconds. A kiss that includes kissing air—that electrically charged space between lovers before physical contact is made which is not dissimilar in effect on our sensibilities as the smell of ozone before rain. In 15 seconds humans are able to determine by smell, then taste and ultimately texture if this tiny intimacy will lead to something more. People who settle for less than an initial kiss of this calibre are surely willing to settle for less in all the little and big things which make up the totality of our lives. Don't settle. Ever.

Our sons and daughters, nieces and nephews, children of friends, and perhaps even grandchildren hear the refrain "you aren't old enough" to date, know what love is, get married, live together—the refrain dates from time immemorial. Pshhaah, I beg to differ with ALL of you naysayers. What I believe is really at play here is that adults do not want to admit they have 'kids' old enough to recognise something more than, as Donny Osmond sang it (I am dating myself here), "*and they call it puppy love.*" If you have provided your offspring, or been an influencing adult, with any amount of nurturing environment and an example (or two) as what love should be—believe me they absolutely know what they feel in their heads and their hearts. They are often times smart enough to wait until chronology and life synch-up to act on it.

I went to a therapist, although he might actually have been a psychiatrist, only once, when I was 17 or 18 years old. It was my mother's idea—she took me, and sat in on the session. I honestly do not recall what the rationale behind the visit was but I do recall the outcome. I wasn't crazy. I knew what I wanted (actually we all do and, with minor exceptions, I honestly don't believe 'we' need to be in therapy for years, or even contribute to the estimated $35B USD spent annually on a global basis figuring it all out). My decision NOT to attend University of Maryland College Park but to stay in Western New York and attend SUNY College Buffalo was made. Why? Because I was in love—only 'he' didn't know it. I thought if I went away to school it would limit the opportunities to be around and explore possibilities when he was home on leave from the Air Force. Yes, we married. Yes, we divorced. Yes, he is still a dear friend and perhaps my greatest cheerleader and I suppose Stephen knew even then that there was a book waiting to be written by his wife even if she didn't.

I had a marvellous, candid, conversation with a 17 year old male friend of mine recently. Owen now off to Pittsburgh to study pre-med, given a 'pass' on having to take the MCATs should he decide to continue his medical school studies there—it could reasonably be said he is beyond intellectually gifted. He's also polite, thoughtful (parents rejoice that Pandora© is unceremoniously changed when an 'ugly word' is part of the lyrics and your toddler is nearby), incredibly supportive of my writing as he's been given periodic sneak peeks. I am thrilled that he has chosen to become a 'morning person' finding he accomplishes more and considers himself happier than mere weeks before this effort began in preparation for his 8AM university classes. We were talking about my writing and our mutual friend Kyle's family, living life fully and how some people just seem to have the ability to cram more living into their lives.

I am not sure how it came up but as my beloved ex-husband Stephen had just been deployed to Iraq and despite the fact that we've been divorced 20 years I am still irrationally concerned over this particular tour of duty. Both my ex and I had a miserable nights' sleep the night before he left—we shared email while he was parked at the USO in Philadelphia. The content of that email isn't really all that important but its' existence provided segue to my 'falling in love' story.

I knew with every fibre of my being that I loved Stephen thoroughly from the first moment my girlfriend Eden introduced us.

Stephen was a jock—Varsity track and soccer—who also sang baritone in the choir, with the elite a cappella group and performed in musicals. At 17, Stephen was 6' tall, handsome in a chiseled-jaw-high-cheekbone-dark-hair way, and 186 pounds of pure, gorgeous muscle. In retrospect, as many of us can equally attest, he was blissfully unaware of the power of his physicality and his sexual appeal. He naively didn't understand why women in their 40's were hitting on him when he collected his paper route money. He was, and is, kind and he also lives his life with more personal integrity than any person I have ever known.

He had a penchant for blonds (still does, though he is more likely to admit to simply loving all women) and as a brunette I believed that I was destined to just be his friend. He was my unequivocal guardian angel. Stephen was my champion and defender throughout high school consistently and miraculously appearing at the precise moment something unpleasant was about to happen to me—there were thousands of small incidents that in today's parlance would be considered bullying (mostly by boys). And because he was "a big man on campus" as long as he was around there was never any problem. The truth is that I absolutely knew (at 15) that, despite my rather imposing Polish father and Catholic upbringing, if he wasn't going to be my husband that he certainly would be my first lover (I waited, and waited and waited to make either of those possibilities a reality with the sure knowledge I would have totally chickened out at the thought of the latter).

At 21, after years of pining, dating other boys and some men, being hit on by much older men and maintaining a tenacious grip on my virginity, driving my girlfriends absolutely nuts with my exasperating narrative on his many attributes—something had to give. My dear friend Gina, at the time dating a professional soccer player named Eduardo Azevado ('Al-lo bay-bee'), took matters into her hands with a dime and a phone call. I knew nothing about until the deed had been done. Returning to our table at T.G.I. FRiDAY'S® after allegedly going to the ladies room Gina said, "You have to promise me if he figures it out you have to tell him everything."

Gina, what have you done?

"I called Stephen. All I said was, 'isn't there someone you should see before you leave tomorrow' and I hung up."

Oh God.

"Promise, Terri."

It seemed a safe bet he wouldn't figure it out so, at about 3:30 in the afternoon, I agreed. Three hours later, with a sicky green MUDD mask covering my face, wearing an equally attractive Lanz® flannel nightgown and tucked into bed with a 'day-over' (the consumption of alcohol when playing with Gina was always epic), the phone rang and my mother called me to pick up. When faced with a potentially life changing moment somehow you should be more suitably kitted out. Yes, it was Stephen. He didn't mention a thing about the phone call from earlier in the day, just asked if he could take me out for a drink before he left for Minot, North Dakota the next day. When I said yes, he said he'd come down to pick me up in twenty minutes. Never doubt any woman's capability to transform in record time when the proper incentive is placed within reach! Showered, hair shampooed and conditioned, devoid of MUDD, legs shaved, make-up and hair done, silk blouse, wool skirt, hose, heels, and jacket in 19 minutes flat. It SOOOOO can be done!

He dropped his mother's clutch in my parents' driveway—so I had to drive. We went a local restaurant and I stuck to ginger ale given the condition of my stomach and my head from earlier in the day. I never imagined that he would actually mention Gina's phone call, but he did, and I honoured my promise to tell him how I felt, had always felt.

It is an uncomfortable thing to be sitting opposite your hearts' desire knowing in 24 hours he will leave for another 9 months of military service and you are about to pour your soul out. All you do at a moment like that is take a deep breath and be as succinct (not my specialty in such matters) as possible and send up a little prayer that it will all work out exactly as it's supposed to. I started my preamble with "We've been friends a long time…" The conversation concluded with an agreement to remain friends.

You can imagine my surprise when driving him home in the snow he asked to stop at the overlook (we grew up on an island), Air Supply was on the radio, and he shimmied over, took me in his arms and kissed me. Thirty years later it still goes down as one of my personal greatest kisses ever. You know, like in the movie of The Princess Bride© when Peter Falk's character is reading to his grandson? Yea, a kiss like that! A kiss that makes you realise what is possible. What love should taste and feel like, the anticipation of it—all. It sets the bar impossibly high at the same time it ensures that you will never settle for less. A kiss like that—a combination of longing fulfilled, pheromones in harmony and natural ability means that future kisses will measured against it, pale in comparison never achieve the illusive swoon factor then blur and fade almost instantly.

Within two months of this kiss, both birthday and Valentine's Cards arrived. By April, a call came for Easter, when the call ended my paternal grandmother, who was living with us, instructed me to go upstairs to her room and open the trunk at the foot of her bed and bring down the quilt lying on top. "Grandma, it's beautiful." A snow white ground, hand quilted, appliqued and embroidered with red poppies. Red has been my favourite colour since childhood. 'That man is going to be your husband. I made that quilt for you before you were born for when you married. Consider it an early wedding present.' "But it was just a phone call." Grandmothers know things we can't begin comprehend.

A bit more than 9 months later Stephen had completed his four years of active duty and came home. Within 3 days he had proposed and subsequently landed in the hospital for an emergency appendectomy—I would prefer to think the two were not in any way connected—we were married two years later.

As I shared the supporting story to my philosophy about the innate self-awareness which we all possess with my friend Owen I was blessed to have him open his heart and head.

Notwithstanding all of his other attributes, the most telling is Owen's maturity. His professed gratitude that his very best friend has, due to the circumstance of high school dating, never been his girlfriend, was expressed without regret. Yet he holds out the sublime hope, and I sense the inherent knowledge, that this young woman possesses all of the attributes to make her a perfect life partner and wife someday. I truly hope to witness the day when Owen is able to make his current awareness a future reality of unbridled joy— just as Mrs Dwyer shared my own wedding.

For weeks, and then months, on end traverse a hundred miles one way over the Scottish Highland's twisting, turning mountain roads to secure treatment for a cancer that is slowly destroying your husband of forty-eight years as my dear friend Agnes Bowie did. Only to watch your friend and lover and partner slip from you in spite of all medicine and you can do for him to know the full extent of love.

Sit in a sacred sanctuary, regardless of your beliefs or who your Prophet might be, and recognise that love defines what it means when in stone is incised "to the glory of God." If the love you feel is as much spiritual as visceral be truly grateful that any one of these types of love have graced your life.

If you love enough, they never leave you.

19 'on wednesdays we wear pink'
—Mean Girls, Paramount Pictures, 2004

I jested to a friend who was wearing a neon pink cardigan that "I didn't get the memo." Keegan chimed her reply by quoting the Karen Smith character in *Mean Girls*.© I roared with delight.

At the same time I recognise that the compliance of our clothing choices, the way we adorn our bodies has by and large become less about expressing our individuality then belonging. When did we become so conformist? In Western society navy, beige, grey and black have become the palate of choice—and not just in corporate environments, not just our clothing but also our homes and cars.

Diana Vreeland once quipped that pink was the navy blue of India—but why should the vast application of pink be limited to India and very little girls? Ah yes, Victoria's Secret Pink University© sorry, not quite the same thing.

There have been cultural reasons attached to the development of both the sari and the conservative attire of the corporate world. The visual voltage of Electric Blue to Fuchsia and Acid Green, 9 yards of jewel-toned silk glittering with the additional embellishment of woven zari, real silver or gold threads, boteh jegheh (paisley) and borders inches deep making up the pallu often with embroidery rich with sequins and pearls makes Indian women, in traditional dress, much like silken butterflies. Navy blue-clad American women pale by comparison. In my previous corporate identity I came to realise that in combination with my personality my closet of expensive navy blue suits was making me fiercely intimidating to everyone around me. Initially I traded this 'corporate uniform' for float-y silk dresses and then for French-cuffed shirts, silk sarong skirts I made out of antique sari's, mules and fishnets—yes, I wore this look in Fortune 50™ companies and was never asked to 'go home and change.' Rather, I was told (at least a couple of times), 'you are like a breath of fresh air around here.'

I am the least beige person you will ever meet. But for Judy Garland playing Dorothy in *The Wizard of Oz*© I might have been content with blue or purple or pink as a favourite colour but, alas, between the sequins and the supposed magical qualities contained in her ruby red shoes my fate was sealed as soon as Glenda the Good Witch told her to click her heels three times. As a result of Dorothy's improbable journey down the Yellow Brick Road and back to Kansas I have this 'thing' about the colour red.

Where some find an accent of red is enough to wear, to decorate with, and others can't be bothered being enveloped in the colour, I happily 'vibrate' at a much higher frequency with it around. I have never seriously studied Feng shui or chakras but intuitively I get the whole fire, anger, sexual passion thing of red I just can't seem to look at it with any of those attributes. For me it's a colour of absolute unconditional happiness, visually tasting like anise candy canes at Christmas!

I can't be bothered with any lip colour which doesn't border on 1940's screen siren, something deep red with a slightly blue undertone (even my Bert's Bees© lip balm is tinted red). I have spent hours, often in vain, seeking the illusive perfect shade and have resorted to a 3-layer approach to achieving the 'right' colour (ladies reading this if you've been equally flummoxed I can only suggest try playing around with an Ecco Bella© Crimson crayon, Hemp Naturals© Scarlet Fire and Face Secret© Matte Lipstick in FC-MLSC as I get lots of queries and compliments on my "shade of lipstick"). This is by the way the perfect shade to leave lip-prints on love letters and Valentines! And especially for sealing a gift of a book or a card to my niece Kelsey (her brother already wise in the machinations of girls at the age of 4 wiped the offending kiss from his latest gift book). Thirty years on, it seems my lipstick application is still memorable for my best friend from college. A conversation down memory lane with Gina and she reminds me of her fascination with the fact that I never needed a mirror to put on lipstick. I remember my reply always being "my mouth has been in the same place for 20 years I ought to know where it is." But to discover that I am remembered each morning as she puts on her lip-liner with this thought I find to be one of the more delightful blessings of our long friendship.

I found a fabulous vintage silk brocade robe in deep ruby red, hand-made in Hong Kong easily 40 years old and probably more like 60, at a consignment shop for $15! The silk is in perfect condition and though it doesn't fit I brought it home anyway and hung it up on the bedroom door like art. It kind of reminds me of a cocktail dress (the feel) my godmother gave as a little girl to play dress up in, so I touch it each time I pass it as a talisman and I think of my Aunt Jeanne.

As I type this an antique uranium trophy cup vase holds a dozen variously shaded Gerbera daisies with Casa Blanca lilies on my desk in front of me. The brilliant reds scream against the acid yellow—the whites tone down the riot of colour.

Some people start their day with caffeine, and continue long passed two cups. My paternal grandmother was one of those amazing volume consumers never affected by drinking the contents of her 12 cup electric percolator—she slept like a log even taking her last cup at 10PM. I am an anti-caffeine person. It almost isn't safe to be around me any time after I have imbibed as I almost literally bounce off the walls. I feel like I am going to have a heart attack and "wired" should be reclassified as high wired. Even some exquisitely roasted decaf coffees have enough residual caffeine to have me staring at the ceiling at 2AM. As I never really understood the appeal of the taste of coffee, except after a very good meal, I came up with a Plan B for partaking in conversation with friends and business colleagues—my own nearly impossible-to-break-routine which borders on any caffeine Jones which the rest of you might enjoy.

Every morning I brew 2 quarts of my tea to drink cold (it is also great hot!). Someplace north of 20 bags go into a mixture of a 1/2" of unrefined local honey topped off with the contents of my 2 quart tea kettle (which sounds like a train is coming through the kitchen—more happiness). I dilute this by 3, still almost the colour of pomegranate juice, the end result is purply-red, what joy to start the day with such a colour! I drink about a gallon of this a day; two 20-ounce bottles of this during my swim each morning alone. The lifeguards at my pool always thought I was drinking juice and a couple times people 'mentioned' that I was mitigating all my swim efforts by drinking so many empty-caloried 'sports drinks' until I clarified what I have concocted and they taste it. Most recently a woman named Christine asked about it. Half in jest I said it is my fountain of youth; if my modestly researched benefits of each respective herb, fruit and tea found within are to be believed then perhaps I have. She absolutely refused to believe I was 50 and 1/2 years old I finally pulled my driver's license out as validation of my claim. While it is tasty, ridiculously low in calories and high in phytonutrients that help fight all kinds of free radical and immune system disease (note, my Ruby TEAse has not been evaluated by the FDA) it's also about the colour, if it was a brown-y green I might not love it so much but it's so pretty to look at with ice cubes dancing in it!

I have a small collection of something I call Happy Pants. If I am having a borderline day they'll push my equilibrium toward a better place. If I am already in a good mood they make me feel like one of those iridescent soap bubbles blown to the wind wafting along until it bursts! My favourite include a pair from Escada© that I bought at Neiman Marcus© on Final Call™ (honestly I still do not understand how it was that they were still available!) are turquoise cotton jeans strewn with white daisies and red poppies, a pair of pyjama bottoms bought in Scituate, Massachusetts in aqua blue with red lobsters printed on them, and a pair of floral printed Vera Bradley© pinwale cords in maroon, hot pink, white, red, turquoise, and goldenrod. You will either love these or hate them—there doesn't seem to be any middle ground. A couple of girlfriends of mine absolutely HATE THEM! You can see it on their faces when I get out of the car wearing them, or hear it more acutely in their comments. Inevitably someone will stop us when we're out and tell me how much they love them, how the pants made them smile and thank me for brightening their day. Not that I need a license to continue wearing them but it's nice to spread some joy around in our angst filled world.

Ear piercing was once the domain of sailors who had survived the navigation of the entire world or crossed the equator, though earring wearing (by both genders date back to ancient Egyptian and Persian BCE times)—everything old is new again. Tattoos used to be the reserve of males marking their passage into manhood such as Maori warriors, guys who spent time in the military or Hell's Angels.™ Within the last two decades a 'tat' has become more acceptable for just about everyone, marking life's journey on middle age and older women who when asked say they feel more complete having been inked. The art has been elevated from dark blue Semper Fi to fantastical, mythical beasts, cherubs and exhaustive bits of literature inked in scrolling Latin or Chinese characters.

I recently met a plus forty-year old woman whose spiritual journey had taken her to Machu Picchu. She discovered her camera bag with money, tickets, passport, et al, was missing with a mere two hours before she needed to be at the airport for her flight back to the United States. The idea of finding anything lost within the sites' approximately 326 square kilometers takes 'needle in the haystack' to a whole different level. Retracing her steps with a guide turned nothing up, understandably panic starts to set in. Yet in this moment she consciously decided to 'be still,' to let the ancient energy of the place wash over her as she issued a silent prayer for help. Within seconds the guide received a radio call that someone had turned in a camera bag. Collecting her (fully intact) bag leaving Machu Picchu with what she describes as a heightened level of gratitude she looked down as something in the dirt glinted in the afternoon light. She described it as a beautiful solid gold necklace with a hummingbird dangling from it. (Amongst the enormously scaled symbols which make up the estimated 2500 BCE Nazca Lines in Peru is a hummingbird. The Andean people, Nazca, Incas, and Aztecs all, revered the hummingbird. Its mythology and symbolism is connected to living a sweet life (it capably bypasses the tough bitter outer layers of a plant and flower to feed only on nectar), learning the truth of beauty, the magic of living in the moment without looking back with regret, a connection with the Divine focused on conscientiously spreading the joy found within our own hearts. This unknown named she decided to celebrate the astonishing 'coincidences' of that day at Machu Picchu with an emerald, medium blue and black hummingbird tattoo on her stomach in the precise style of the Nazca one—it's breathtaking for all the right reasons.

A little girl runs passed me at the pool, she has on a Little Mermaid™ bathing suit (I would LOVE ONE!), her little friend (perhaps 3 years old) in a hot pink bikini, complete with layers of ruffles on the bottom of her suit like a tiny tutu.

Virtually every young man, and some a little too old to try and carry this look off, sports a pair of jeans four or five sizes too big, at least six inches of their plaid, print or Joe Boxers© showing. A girlfriend age sixty comments that she feels safe with this apparel style because no one could possibly steal her purse and get very far with their pants falling down.

The other day I saw a more than a bit past middle-aged man sitting under an umbrella sporting shocking pink hair! It might not be something most of us would do but I think he was making a statement about having fun, not taking himself or this crazy world too seriously. A heavy set woman riding on a Harley Davidson© wears the company colours of orange and black striped socks, a black skirt and an orange top—or, maybe, it's because Halloween is coming up soon? All I can say is that I noticed!

I can't encourage any of you sufficiently to break the mould to express a personal style that plays up your femininity or masculinity, your outrageous sense of humour, your irreverence, your decision to be a super hero or a faery princess (okay, within reason) but most of all to not comply with some perceived rigid protocol. For goodness sake have a little fun—even if it makes your friends wince!

20 low hanging fruit

During the course of my entire adult life when it has come to 'working out' I have been a slug more frequently than not. The idea of my fitness (or not) being tied to active membership in a health club is laughable. My lack of motivation to get off my butt has never had anything in common with self-loathing, rather was usually was work-related. When I have been remarkably fit the only thing that was different about me was that I made the time to feel the sensual pleasures of the wind in my hair and the accompanying the physicality of swimming, sailing, down-hill skiing or cycling to transcend (downward) my 'normal' size 12 (or larger) person.

We're all going to approach exercise differently but just as Epictetus (AD 55—AD 135) said, 'If one oversteps the bounds of moderation, the greatest pleasures cease to please.'

At 28, suddenly 40 pounds heavier than the day of my wedding six years earlier, faced with being single and with the reality of very likely never being a mom, you can count on the fact I was miserable and terrified. I have always had this theory that if you are afraid of something you need to do something a little scarier—in this case it was the idea of breaking my leg (or neck) and those 'little ant people' at the bottom of the hill. To get through my divorce, I learned to ski.

Try hiring an instructor when you are approaching 30 and overweight and now wearing five layers of clothes to stay warm (because you aren't moving fast enough to do otherwise). Handsome, beautiful 20 year old man-boys, trying to make the US Ski Team© do not teach older women to ski; they are either trying to attract the attention of pink angora and white stretch pants clad snow bunnies or they are trying to shave 10 seconds off their run.

At the beginning, when I could get barely get myself down the bunny-hill or the Green Circles, I hyperventilated and subsequently had muscle spasms because our bodies really do need oxygen to function properly, an incredible man named Jack O'Brian (age 72 in 1989) took pity on me. Jack said he learned on wooden skis and the tuck and roll wipe-out method. He graciously offered to ski with me, not teach, thereby avoiding the private lesson tuition I could ill-afford. Three days a week, every week for the duration of the season, until the school ski clubs arrived, we skied. I would bake something (I think he had lost his wife so my baking was home-style comfort) and bring it along. We would meet in the lodge, have breakfast together and then be the first ones up the lift and down the hill. In 10 weeks Jack had me on Black Diamond terrain, and I was (most likely from the rush of fear induced adrenaline) down 30 pounds.

When spring 1989 came, I found someone to teach me to sail in exchange for my being 'rail weight' and scrubbing the boat clean. Skipper April said I had the most natural ability to feel the wind direction and point up the boat in the many decades she had been on the water (isn't it just so nice to have a 'natural aptitude' for something?). We night sailed within a fortnight, and she didn't hesitate to give me the helm for ½ the journey. Above us a billion dazzling stars on a pitch black sky, a swath of the Milky Way and a breeze that was letting me coax 5 knots out of the Catalina© (top hull speed was 7). 22 years later I can still relive the sensation of this summer night.

I am 'present' in every moment, what matters is only right now, not last week, not next year, but right now. How fully can I experience the dawn of each new day? Fill it up, regardless of how mundane it might appear? This mindfulness allows me to capture life's beautiful subtlety that eclipses notice of most of us rushing through the day. While this is my reality, there isn't one person on this planet for whom living in sensual pleasure isn't possible.

Six weeks later the Tall Ship, the HMS Bounty arrived in Buffalo at Erie Basin Marina and while I might not have known what 'The Bounty' was at the moment that it was suggested we go see her, I fell instantly and passionately in love standing next to all 169' of her hand made copper-clad hull and miles of linen canvas. There is this moment in a throng of others equally smitten where my voice is heard to say 'So, are you ever looking for crew?' Hey, I was going through a divorce. There are probably less significant reasons for running away to the sea. In fact it didn't quite turn out that way.

'Low hanging fruit' is a salesman's term for sales opportunities that do not require a lot of effort to close. Low hanging fruit is like reaching up into the tree of life, and plucking a rose tinted apple then biting down, your mouth filling with crisp delicious apple flesh and the sun-warmed juice racing across your tongue. Life can be exactly like that but it does take practice. I think it's important to recognise that we build our life successes incrementally. With each new role we assume there will be skills and confidence building challenges which prepare us for competence at the next level. Even with the greatest qualifications on the Earth there are social and cultural aptitudes, personal appearance and emotional grace to master. Baby steps don't cease to be relevant to our growth at age 2. No matter how much we think we know as we graduate from college most of us won't walk into a corner office and a CEO title. Building our resume is more than entry level job to middle management to vice president and eventually C-level role just as being a great spouse doesn't come immediately following being a boy/girlfriend for the first time or being a great lover after a first kiss or being a wonderful parent just happen because you had parents or took on that role as a child because your family dynamic demanded that you step in to fill the void. Not so suddenly you come to realise that everything you have ever done has laid the groundwork to ensure that you at least know how to do what you are about to take on and hopefully ensure your success.

If you don't know something, or think you do but it might be wiser to garner a second opinion, there's no shame in seeking out someone who can guide your growth in the precise area which is giving you some measure of pause. Executive and athletic coaches, sports psychologists, etiquette experts, stylists (both fashion and hair), spiritual leaders, and teachers of all kinds exist, make their livelihood, to help all of us achieve our personal best.

Do something a just little hard to gain your confidence. Build on that successful experience with subsequent levels of difficulty, or ease, so that when it really counts (when you 'think' you are intimidated beyond belief, scared senseless of possible failure, all the cards are riding on your next decision) you somehow muster the ability to press on and tackle the tough stuff of life.

I couldn't tell you what possessed me to feel that I had the competency to even apply to become the Operations Manager for the HMS Bounty. I couldn't tell you where I found the inspiration to research Admiralty Law dating back to John Paul Jones and subsequently write a business plan for shifting her away from status as a moored attraction as a (very big) movie prop and being foreign-flagged she could not 'sail for hire' in US coastal waters without (expensive) Merchant Mariners as crew. I have no idea where I got the absolute nerve, when after four months of hanging loose, to (nicely) demand an interview with the senior management of Turner Broadcasting (including the CFO and Ted's best friend from grade school) all the while listening to my parents daily degrading comments to my ambition and repeatedly suggesting that I just get a waitressing job. Perhaps for no other reason than I knew I had the skills to do the job and that I *needed* to beat out the other 150 candidates with Coast Guard and Naval experience to prove, mostly to myself, that my soon to be ex-husband was right in suggesting that he just "wanted someone ordinary" because I was anything but ordinary. If he wanted to give me my wings to fly then I was going to do my damnedest to prove him right—there wasn't anything I couldn't do!

Inside all of us is an internal clock mechanism that sounds a resonant chime when something feels right. This intuition of ours is steeped in our evolutionary origins; it's the adrenaline coursing through our veins to fuel our success at coming back alive from hunting Mastodon and it still relevant today tens of thousands of years on in mankind's development to live well and leave the world a better place than it was when we came into it.

If we 'listen' to that intuition and apply our passion to our goals with a fierce determination we all can earn a place of sweet victory.

Try something you never thought you even wanted to do!

Go pick the tree of life. Then tomorrow—reach a little higher tomorrow.

21 nice is as nice does

Is there anyone having seen Julie Andrews spinning around with her arms outstretched on that beautiful hilltop playing Maria von Trapp, singing, "*the hills are alive with the sound of music,*" who hasn't smiled to themselves that life could be so fully joyful?

I maintain that my singular role in the universe is to leave the room lighter than when I came into it—it's not always easy. Not everyone responds positively, some people seem utterly incapable of smiling or laughing, but that doesn't mean I am going to cease trying. Saying something nice or doing nice isn't hard to do, giving a smile away is a pretty simple thing to do.

There are a hundred profound delights to be found in the charming French film starring Omar Sharif as *Monsieur Ibrahim*© and Pierre Boulanger; not the least is the life lesson Sharif's character imparts to his protégé played by Boulanger about the value of smiling. Rent it. Enable the subtitle feature even if you speak French. Watch it twice before returning. Believe me, so much about what I am trying to convey here in **All That I Need** can be found within that movie.

See a great tie on a gentleman? tell him—even if his wife is standing next to him, a four-year-old in a ruffled tutu skirt? Oh yea, you bet I tell her how beautiful she looks and how I would LOVE TO HAVE a skirt just like hers! Or LED-lit sneakers on a little boy? Yep. Fabulous meal? If I don't walk into the kitchen (and believe me I have) I convey my desire to meet the chef or ask my waiter to "please go kiss the chef fully on the mouth for me." Gorgeous hair? Beautiful eyes? Outrageous pair of shorts? Fabulously wild sneakers that turn out to glow in the dark? Yes, yes. YES! I draw the line at compliments about physical attractiveness because of an indelibly imprinted on my brain lesson learned at 20 that I can only attribute the comment to youthful naïveté, and I do not recommend repeating it. I offer it here as an example of 'what not to say.'

As indicated previously I held a sales clerk role at a carriage trade retailer in my youth. The store offered beautiful, and expensive, things. Our customers would be unlikely to cross the threshold of either JC Penny© or Target.© Working one day an absolutely gorgeous man, probably in his 40's, was browsing the racks. He was so amazing looking anyone would have noticed, but it slipped from my mouth in what I thought was the tiniest whisper, "Oh. Hurt Me." As luck would have it the gentleman's wife was standing behind me, and clearly thought this sassy young thing was going to make a play for her man. Truly, I wasn't. I was simply admiring his man-beautiful person, the same as I would any piece of art. Within five minutes I was called to the store managers' office. Hilda demanded an explanation, my face beet red with embarrassment, I tried to explain. As she had seen the couple she just laughed loudly as it was so clear to her I had no idea what I had said. When she explained how my words had been taken I flushed an even deeper shade of red. The only response to be made was the truth… she should be delighted that he was her man!

Make the over-stressed cashier laugh? YES! By example, I was returning an item to Marshall's© and noticed a package of Gummi® 'fried eggs' near the register. I commented that would make a great Father's Day breakfast. The woman looked at me puzzled.

Well, I said. Mother's Day comes a month before Father's Day, right?

Yes, she said.

So put Gummi eggs, Begging Strips® bacon dog treats, et al on a plate to celebrate and when he complains that it's all fake you smile brightly and reply 'But dear so were the pearls you gave me for Mother's Day!'

I thought she was going to split her sides, she couldn't have been more grateful. How much easier this made the transaction for both of us and the break in her day. I left the room lighter, mission accomplished.

For all that I find it easy find the humour in the mundane or to pay compliments it's more difficult, and embarrassing, for me to receive them. I don't think this a bad thing to have our self-image 'in check' to the degree that we can be normal and a hat still fits on our head.

I was chatting with a friend at the end of one of my swim work-outs about trying beat the effects of being in the pool for a couple hours each day and grow my hair out because just once in my life I would like to look like a romance novel heroine. The not-so-attractive look of silicone Speedo cap helps—mine is 'as cute' as possible in a blue and yellow tie-dye pattern but still no one looks great in bathing caps. A few mornings later a woman that had been in an adjacent lane told me, "I saw you in the locker room with your hair done and lipstick on, don't underestimate how beautiful you already are." At that moment, perhaps because someone unknown to me provided validation of my attractiveness, I found my perspective shifted and just as suddenly men who collectively have paid scant attention to me over the last six years seemed to be actively hunting me.

Once I become your friend I will defend you and your heart even to your own sabotaging, so it should come as no surprise that being gracious in the face of betrayal is not something I do well. In a society that increasingly is focused upon the self, this character trait of mine can be a good thing or a bad thing. Maybe loyalty is out of date? My maternal grandfather used to say "if you don't have something nice to say, better to not say anything at all" and "you don't hate. You might dislike them intensely but you don't hate anyone." When we're young it's drilled into our heads to 'treat others as you'd like to be treated.' If adults remembered that more often maybe we'd have less divorce, less neurosis, possibly even less war and murder. There's a reason we shouldn't air all our most private details and dirty laundry to even someone we consider a 'best' friend because anger and resentment are a breeding ground for contemptuous behaviour. It needn't, or perhaps shouldn't be that way.

I was trying (really hard) to be mindful of all this at the second marriage of a dear friend and her amazing new husband. A certain 'friend' of the bride-to-be with whom I am only mildly acquainted, threatened to put the kibosh on the happy couple early in their relationship with the verbal equivalent of a tell-all book venomously spewed about the woman's past for the benefit of protecting the man involved. We are not talking about teenagers or twenty-something's, all three individuals have earned every grey hair on their heads or chins—even if they colour. I felt, still feel, that the rather distasteful, remarkably inappropriate and insensitive attempts to thwart blossoming love warranted exclusion from the wedding. I freely acknowledge it was not my place but it didn't seem to make much sense to me include someone in the celebration who wasn't cheering the couple on from the very beginning.

As it had been over 18 months since we'd been in the same room I wasn't even sure I would recognise this alleged friend of my friends if she was invited, in fact I didn't. To be sure it's a lot awkward when someone hugs you and you don't know who it is. More so when it does finally dawn on you that the someone who has just touched you is someone whose behaviour you find untenable. Thankfully there was almost 3 hours between ceremony and reception for my mental recovery. Rather than be rude or call this person out and make a scene I simply excused myself (like I was going to the ladies room) and left my table when this person decided to plop down next to me. Yes, it was the path of least resistance and no, it didn't make me feel great to do it, but at the risk of escalation to making a scene this was decidedly the better choice. I could hear my grandfather in my head, "if you don't have something nice to say . . ."

22 who are you?

Bottega Veneta© launched their eponymous tagline "when your own initials are enough™" in the 1970's. I so agree, with a solid sense of self, regardless of your personal accomplishments, no one (should) need to wear a logo to establish their arrival in the world. I think this axiom should go a little further though as everyone puts their pants on the same way why should what someone does (or the club they belong to or subsequently how much money they have) be more important than 'who' they are inside?

I spent a year working as a shift supervisor for Starbucks.© My experience there made one thing very clear, the sense of entitlement of the people taking two parking spots with their Porsches© or Hummers,© who also never left a tip despite that their very specific specialty drink was often ready for them before they even got to the cashier, fall into the seriously misguided or perhaps just overly wounded category. No matter how accomplished they might be these people have not learned that 'the trappings' are far less important that than substance. You listen to them go on and on about how much the house down the street just sold for, how much their new car cost, watch their conspicuous consumption mount into the frenzy of keeping up. Why is it that the car you drive, the zip code in which you live, the title on your business card, or the amount of 'bling' adorning you, or your spouse, is more important that kindness, integrity, compassion, and competency as a human being? You are truly blest when you understand that things and money are fleeting and should never take superior position over relationships and love.

Our global society has become obsessed with celebrity, why would being infamous for accomplishing nothing be more desirable than becoming a quiet hero to even one other person? The plaque on the building or on the wall of the hospital, the park bench, the list of patrons for the Philharmonic all very nice but are we donating our wealth and time because we passionately believe in the rightness of the cause or to earn recognition? Charity is not something merely to claim on itemized tax returns or for bragging rights, rather it should be about diminishing a tiny bit of pain and suffering, disease or agony in the world. It should be about giving as much as your heart possibly can. In writing this I am reminded of a lesson learned, without the following scripture involved, by The Reverend Monsignor Richard Graber who was given one of my parents' Cocker Spaniels when I was seven years old and eventually married me many years later. In essence, if what you do requires the accolades of others then you are not acting of benevolence but rather to satisfy your ego.

Be careful not to do your 'acts of righteousness' before men, to be seen by them. If you do, you will have no reward from your Father in heaven. So when you give to the needy, do not announce it with trumpets, as the hypocrites do in the synagogues and on the streets, to be honored by men. I tell you the truth, they have received their reward

in full. But when you give to the needy, do not let your left hand know what your right hand is doing, so that your giving may be in secret. Then your Father, who sees what is done in secret, will reward you.
—Matthew 6:1-4

If I have it I share. If I don't have it I will find a way to somehow overcome my poverty to still make an occasion special for someone I love. I FREELY admit I can be a little ambivalent about money and I can honestly say that have never balanced my checkbook. I have (rather rudely) slapped $5 in front of someone who didn't need it just to get her to shut up after three weeks of whining about how expensive it was to incorporate or trademark or whatever. (I could ill afford to this.) If I can't make things equal monetarily I will try to balance things out with my time. It's not about, as my father would comment, "not owing anyone anything", it's more about pulling my weight in a relationship and there are a million ways to accomplish this.

I had a manic (and perhaps a bit mad) boyfriend for a short time (everyone else around me surely felt it was longer) whose unwillingness to spend money was legendary. He existed on coffee and candy and while he would begrudgingly pay for my meal he wouldn't eat himself, he would walk instead of taking public transportation (which of course is fine unless you are the date in 4" heels). He finagled with his taxes—receipts for businesses that were paper only and which conducted no actual commerce so the United States government always wound up owing him money. He objected not one bit to enjoying hospitality and comfort from other people but would wear the same clothes day after day and lived in an embarrassing hovel of less than 900 square feet on 3 floors with at least 3 'immigrant tenant' room-mates (from whom he collected cash rents) infested with mice and roaches. More maddening than every one of these eccentricities was that every nickel spent was accounted for, demanded repayment and belaboured as if it was his last. I never kept a chit record of who bought what when until dating this man—I learned to keep receipts. It was always interesting when he brought out his Excel spreadsheet with the "I paid for this" and convenient memory lapse against all that I paid for.

Perhaps the buy and buy and buy (or save and save and save) people think there's something wrong with the rest of us. Unless its money or some degree of precious against an unattainable scale of validation nothing provides value to some people. Their spouses and children only serve as props against perceived success, status symbols rather than individuals whose desires and needs are tertiary to maximising a hunger for recognition. Let's buy the kids wide screen, plasma TV's for their bedrooms but avoid getting home on time to take them to the Doctor.

The other extreme of this is "penny wise and pound foolish", we all know people who apply the axiom of frugality to such an extreme as to live with bare refrigerators, their cars barely passing inspection and threadbare clothing so they can justify spending money on country club memberships, foreign destination golf outings, and long weekends with the boys fishing, or 'bling' to assert their arrival in society.

What does all this accomplish? I believe only a false sense of personal identity, envy, greed, lust, competitiveness with everyone trying to be 'the best' (at whatever) rather than happiness. Like the old fable of Midas' gold which only proved to destroy lives rather than enrich them the lesson will eventually be learned. I can't tell you how to re-align yourself but, simple pleasures which cost next to nothing like simply sitting next to water and watching seagulls soar, picking up bits of sea glass to remember a day of sublime perfection are precious.

Learn to appreciate the value of quiet and nature, your place in the world without the relentless pursuit of validation from other people based solely upon your net worth.

23 surprise and delight

Most of us have little expectation of tender expressions coming our way on a regular basis; which can make being on the receiving end a little difficult at times. Being good at being the recipient takes some measure of practice unless you are a mercenary bitch or a kept man.

But giving doesn't really take a lot to get it right—it simply takes a good dose of thoughtfulness, a little style and a sense of timing; something we would all do well to remember. Some people are incredibly talented at this—they read you like a book, listen to what you are saying, remember long after you've forgotten, act on it to create delight.

For the occasion of our engagement my husband bestowed me with a copy of the c.1981-1885 BCE faïence hippopotamus affectionately referred to as William who resides at the Metropolitan Museum of Art in New York City. I had coveted William since the 10th grade, about the same time I truly fell in love with Stephen, so his knowledge of me in the form of this turquoise pottery beast said more than any diamond might have. Years later, and obviously post-divorce, William has lost none of his charm but now has friends,

Gilbert and Philippe, which were purchased at The Met and the Louvre, but named by my niece Julia. Her gift of their naming on a Christmas morning after our brunch is just as precious to me as something physically tangible.

My niece Kelsey made a tempera painting of herself in pre-K and gifted it to me; her funny 3 year old expressionist view of herself in shades of pink and yellow and jade green hangs in my kitchen in a pink frame. At the same age her younger brother Michael Logan made a snowman door mat out of a carpet square remnant that his mom seriously wanted, "No mommy, for AuntTe." I confess I only put the snowman out at Christmas-time so he stays nice for a very long time. These gifts are especially cherished for the innocence of childhood and the unconditional love and thoughtfulness which they represent.

I will never forget my niece EJ's 12th birthday. I lived in Cambridge, MA, at the time. She hadn't specifically asked (and I swear I didn't "know") but I knew she had a retro 60's and 70's thing going on at the time so I sent her the nearly 8 pound tome, The Beatles Anthology. There is an instant replay running in my head at this moment. Her adolescent voice echoes in the hallway and sound of her feet pounding down the stairs come simultaneously to my ear as her mom calls her to tell her I am on the phone. Her screaming enthusiasms of "I LOVE IT! I love it, I love it. THAAANNK YOOOUUU SOOOO MUCH AUNT TERRI" make their way to my ears 400 miles away. Ah, Music. I get her verbal hug. For her 16th birthday I drive in from Connecticut. Take her to a big box electronics store where I have reserved the first generation iPod™ for her. The shock and delight cannot be measured. As a sophomore at University of Pennsylvania bought me a book entitled *The Complete Book of Aunts* by Rupert Christiansen which might just be the smallest yet grandest thank you I have ever received.

For Christmas one year my dearest friend Doris handed me a box which literally fit in the palm of my hand—its weight totally illogical to its size. We sat at her round beige and white Formica kitchen table opening one another's presents and I tried to figure out what could possibly weigh so much and be so tiny. When I exhausted my three guesses and finally opened the box I discovered nestled inside one of her very old, perfectly beautiful bronze Buddha's; an unusual double happiness Buddha standing, laughing, with money purses not in one but in both upraised hands. To me there is nothing as precious as a gift which because of its' long ownership by someone you love contains their energy.

Though we see one another infrequently at best our friendship spanning more than thirty years is a treasure in and of itself. Dora and I worked in the same store as 19-year-olds, attended the same university. It's her moms' recipe for Moussaka that I use when I have to 'have it' rather than rely upon a Greek diner to do the dish proper justice. But a casual conversation a little over a year ago is the basis of one of the most heartfelt gifts ever 'presented' to me; Dora simply said that every time she drove passed the church where I was married she offers up prayer and asks God to bless me. Somehow that someone loves me sufficiently to ask for the Divine's grace to wash over me makes the gratitude for all my life's blessings just that much profound.

You wouldn't think a facsimile transmission could find merit as a treasure. When I arrived at my hotel in Budapest the day of my 39th birthday awaiting me were faxes and birthday cards, Champagne and flowers universally sent by friends back in Boston so that I wouldn't be alone on my special day. That some of this effort would have required mailing weeks in advance made the thoughtfulness involved the truest blessings I have ever received.

My friend Greg and I always share a double pour of The Macallan© 25-year old to celebrate all that we have missed in one another's lives when our schedules finally allow us to catch up someplace in Scotland or in New York City. Somehow my friend of many years Dan remembered my ordering the same before dinner out one night and many months later bought me a bottle for Christmas– I made it last the entire year enjoying it only in celebration of life's most cherished moments. For my 50th birthday my friends Pam and Bruce bought me a lovely (chic) bottle of French Champagne yet un-drunk. I await the university acceptance letters for my nieces Kate and Julia to share this in celebration with them and their parents.

I have no idea why this became important, but on the eve of my divorce I vowed I would never wear costume jewelry again. I had a ring made in Atlanta during the emotional roller coaster year of my separation and I still wear it in front of my great grandmothers' wedding band on my pinkie finger. The yellow gold ring features a period coin of the emperor Constantine in profile and is set with small pave diamonds. Compliments over the years continue to be met with the pronouncement made on initially placing it on my finger "the only man worth having is one wrapped around my little finger." Okay, I was a little bitter and needed time to heal. The ring now serves as a token reminder that whatever hurts will, eventually, heal.

Fifteen years later a man listened intently. Because I had not yet found one he gave me an antique glass pickle ornament for my Christmas tree—in more charming, less abundant times, a child finding this ornament was entitled to an extra gift. He sent Neuhaus chocolates by UPS© (insane). Unbeknownst to me he schemed and colluded with the owners of stores that I patronised, and purchased a gold, seed pearl and faceted garnet brooch that I was looking forward to purchasing on my own. He doubled it up by having it placed within an enormous bouquet of white roses, heather, birch twigs, and thistles. The shop owner called me and asked me to stop by and visit (I thought to have me reconcile my account a little overdue). I recall the phone ringing repeatedly and her ignoring it, finally apologising for the delay in delivering a bouquet to me with the frenzy of Valentine's Day. Before I even opened the card, my florist friend chirped "there's a box from a jeweller too, I had to sign for it!" My so face betrayed my emotions she gasp and said, "You don't love him do you?" "No. No, I don't." Eventually I came to understand his gift was purely one of respect and love and yet, at the time I was angry at the presumption and for his taking away my purchasing independence. The Anise Gumdrop, as I refer to it, has become something more than what it was. It marks my heart with the knowledge that once someone tried really hard to bring me, and only me, a fanciful but lasting token of love and I didn't know how to receive the gift with grace. I am most guilty of scorning one of the most special gifts ever bestowed upon me—I am still trying to make it a little less wrong a whole bunch of years later.

My mother used to say it was impossible to buy me anything because I just buy what I want. That wasn't (entirely) true, but getting a gift right isn't about you, it's about the receiver. The giver needs to really understand the recipient, who they are and celebrating them. A gift given which merely fills the void because 'something' needs to presented isn't really a gift—is it?

Touching a person you love at their essence with something unique to them is almost an art form. It's never about the quantity of the presents or about the amount of money spent (or it shouldn't be) but a kindness that leaves both the giver and the recipient somewhat breathless and satiated with mutual delight.

24 time to say goodbye

I went to the woods because I wished to live deliberately, to front only the essential facts of life, and see if I could not learn what it had to teach, and not, when I came to die, discover that I have not lived.
—Henry David Thoreau 1817-1862

Not tragic to die doing what you love. You want the ultimate thrill, you gotta be willing to pay the ultimate price."
—Patrick Swayze, as Bodhi, Point Break© 1991

What would be tragic, as my long ago ski buddy John noted, is to live life 'in bland pastel.'

From star to garden slug what makes each exist is eternal and enduring, only its present state before us is fleeting. Epicurus (341 -271 BCE) wrote eloquently of beginnings and endings, a constant state of decline and renewal based upon the finite mass which makes up our universe:

And so the destructive motions cannot hold sway eternally and bury existence forever;
nor again can the motions that cause life and growth preserve created things eternally.

It must be realised by mankind in total, and in particular the individuals who make up our immediate circle of influence, that we truly are connected as mass and in energy. When friends are sad, or happy, nothing connects us to them faster than a hug. When presented with human misery we reach out to offer assistance and compassion.

Others would surely argue, but I believe it is the knowing, the intellectual comprehension of how our universe functions when coupled with acute observation which shifts our perception of the mundane to absolute wonder.

Rise before dawn to be first on the beach to glean the bits of detritus launched upon the shores by the push and pull of the moon's cycles. Tuck into the tidal pools hugged by rocks, the rush of waves spilling their contents within and rediscover in the calm between those waves what it is like to be a toddler at the beach for the first time. The shard of cobalt blue sea glass you've just found was once a bottle until it outlived its original purpose and was cast into the sea. There, amidst the tumult of elements, raging waters dense with salt the bottle churned against rock and reef breaking it into ever smaller pieces. Smoothed by the very silica from which the bottle was created by man deploying technology, its edges and surface being reclaimed bit by tiny bit until all that remains is a piece of glass the size of a fingernail, smoothed by years of ebbing tides which appears at your feet. Why do we as humans discard the original bottle yet cherish the tiny fragment of its former self? Does knowing what it was mitigate or enhance the delight in finding it? As someone whose own efforts sometimes pluck the sensual soft shards of polished green, aqua, pale amethyst, blue, cobalt, once clear and now frosted glass from ocean beaches far and wide I know that what I cherish is the connection to the impossible journey that brought this 'treasure' to me. That it still remains and is now in my hand is chance of discovery and infinite possibility.

I intellectually understand the eternal cycle of creation and dissolution of both the bottle and my own being. But if I touch and treasure these fleeting bits, notice a yellow swallowtail and capture it in my head and heart rather than pin it to velvet and mount it under glass, delight in the chalk drawings of my niece and nephew before the clouds burst with abundance and wash it all away yet lift my face toward the heavens and feel the cool drops of water on my face and skin, I experience the cycle of renewal and impermanence and bathe in the pleasure of each cycle.

I probably spend more time driving along desolate, single-track roads in Scotland than I do on Interstates in the United States. For me, besides being a means of getting to where I have promised, or need, to be these drives are at once serene and intoxicating. There, cutting through the primeval landscape, stone millions and millions of years old, rushing waters cut channels, drop and cascade through ravines according to primal force eventually finding dry stone beds and then filling the banks to overflowing, at certain times of the year it really is possible to become one with the universe. Sometimes the roads over mountains are blocked with snow when they should be clear, or fog cascades dense as a forest making a drive in Boston rush hour seem like a walk through its Public Gardens. You can easily find yourself along the edge of a sea loch, literally less than a metre separating you and the car from a drop the height of a several storied tall building; having driven them both ways I offer that it's infinitely better in pitch darkness not to know exactly where you are (if you think these roads are lit by anything more than your headlights and the moon you are crazier than I am for actually driving them). When you are on the west coast of Scotland or up in her islands (where, *if there is a signpost* it's in Gaelic or Faroese and your map is in English with teeny weeny Gaelic or Faroese bracketed below) you make darn sure you have a tank of gas, a bag of Clementine's, bottled water and a roll of toilet paper in the back seat! Of course it's nothing as perilous as what Ewan McGregor documented in crossing into former Soviet Bloc countries riding his motorcycle with his best mate around the world but there is a certain 'no one really knows where I am, I neglected to check-in' aspect to the drive that certainly adds to my exhilaration.

We should live for moments which humble us, which grant a sense of awe that can only be described as reverence. Be astonished, yet again, at the measure of physical accomplishment by Dana Torres or Michael Phelps, or the impossible odds against success being realised by the 1980 United States Men's Hockey Team. You let your eye fully absorb magnificence the way my very talented friend Iain Clark is able to do with his camera and then turn it into something better in his head as art for the rest of us to enjoy, of a sunrise (or sunset), the fleeting seconds around a child's breath sending a cloud dandelions on the wind, an end of summer butterfly wafting on air currents and you quiet your mind; as one of my friend Doug Leclair's favourite bands so aptly captured (lyrics abbreviated):

I feel the change
Goin' on all around me
It's strange
How I'm taken and guided
Where I end up right I'm needed to be
[Chorus]
At the end of the water
A red sun is risin'
And the stars are all goin' away
And if you're too busy talkin'
You're not busy listenin'
To hear what the land has to say

 213

I hear the waves
Sun beatin' down on my shoulders
It's a near-perfect day
Wishin' I wouldn't get any older
They say that it's gone 'fore you know it and
Soak it all in
— "Quiet your mind,©" The Zack Brown Band

You'll have your own special place—a cabin in the woods, a lake cottage, a ski con-do—located anywhere. For me it's the elemental beauty to be found in Scotland which beckons me back over and over again to reclaim myself, calm my central nervous system down from the constant assault of contemporary life and observe nature's magnificence, be a little terrified of driving across glens where intuitively I 'feel' something very bad hap-pened like it was yesterday (only to research it later to have my suspicions confirmed) see Osprey and Roe deer bucks at the height of rutting season, and tiny beggars, robins so tame they harass you into giving them food and will eat from your hands.

When you drive amidst such a landscape you have plenty of time to just think. Often times there is no reception to be had on the car radio—the mineral content and sheer mass of Scotland's mountains serves to block signals remarkably well—and if there's nothing to slide into the CD player then it's whatever esoteric thoughts decide to rifle through my brain. For as long as I can remember one absolute of mine has been to not just think, but to believe with a surety which would make insurance companies deny me a policy should I ever apply for coverage, that I would not live to see my hair turn grey. When you 'know' something like that (dearest friends reading this, be assured there is no medical evidence to validate my theory) you live differently. You belt out songs on the radio with conviction, even if it's the wrong key at times, and embrace the ideas put for in Tim McGraw's song, "Live Like You Were Dying©" (lyrics abbreviated):

He said I was in my early 40's,
With a lot of life before me,

And a moment came that stopped me on a dime.
I spent most of the next days, lookin' at the x-rays,
Talkin' 'bout the options and talkin' 'bout sweet time.
Asked him when it sank in, that this might really be the real end.
How's it hit ya, when you get that kind of news.
Man what ya do.
And he says,
I went sky divin,'
I went rocky mountain climbin,'
I went 2.7 seconds on a bull name Fu Man Chu.
And I loved deeper,
And I spoke sweeter,
And I gave forgiveness I've been denying,
And he said someday I hope you get the chance,
To live like you were dyin.'

When you understand that filling your days like a cup to overflowing up shouldn't be because you have a diagnosis with a finite amount of time, but rather because there's exists within you the singular recognition that from the day of our births we are all on an irrevocable path with death, you take nothing for granted. You fill yourself up with the mundane and precious, you worry less and try not to control sheer nothingness, you make yourself accessible, you love, laugh and cry freely, the passions of your mind and body have nothing to do with the negative, and real beauty can be found in everything around us if our powers of observation are honed to razor sharpness.

You stop the car and, however inappropriately you might be dressed, climb a muddy winding path up to the top of a promontory in the Kyle of Lochalsh to see the view and pay respects at a World War I memorial represented by a somber kilted Macrae carved of granite perched above Loch Duich and visually equal with the Five Sisters of Kintail. Closer to angels and God is certainly possible in Scotland but certainly not in a silk skirt.

You stand before the names etched onto the black marble surface of the Vietnam War Memorial or the red leather books which name every fallen hero of Scottish blood within the Scottish National War Memorial and try to absorb the evidence of how fleeting life can be—all that remains for the rest of us are the names of someone's loved ones. You issue prayer for those unknown souls to be bathed in quiet peace.

You drive out of your way to stop at the Lake of Menteith and in the dead of winter, ice still floating on the surface, and walk into the crystal clear water just because you can. If you are riding your bike you do so without your helmet because in truth if you are going to be hit, or fall, wouldn't it be better to have 'what's useful' gleaned from our bodies, to give others this precious gift of life than to be vegetable material or physically confined to a bed or wheelchair the rest of our lives?

Both Epicurus (341-271 BCE) and Brian Greene (1963-) eloquently captured the dynamics of the universe; all events are ultimately based purely upon the activity of atoms moving within a (very large) empty space—particle entanglement as its' known. There are no gods, nor a singular God in our monotheistic cultures, to reward or punish humans as the whole universe is infinite and eternal—they have better things to do, like enjoy themselves! Epicurus, in his letter to Menoeceus, wrote, "So we must exercise ourselves in the things which bring happiness, since, if that be present, we have everything, and, if that be absent, all our actions are directed towards attaining it."[…] "He who has a clear and certain understanding of these things will direct every preference and aversion toward securing health of body and tranquillity of mind, seeing that this is the sum and end of a blessed life." Clearly he didn't believe death was to be feared, famously writing in the same letter, "…therefore a correct understanding that death is nothing to us makes the mortality of life enjoyable, not by adding to life a limitless time, but by taking away the yearning after immortality." If there is, and I do believe as much, some kind of Divine then I made my peace a long time ago; s/he could take me tomorrow and I would have no regret and, perhaps, because of this belief I have no fear of dying.

Humanists for thousands of years, and Physicists more recently, have recognised, made peace with, and attempted to live life fully and completely in the recognition that in the end we are the same atoms, mere particles of dust, which make up our universe.

I close my eyes, only for a moment, and the moment's gone
All my dreams, pass before my eyes, a curiosity
Dust in the wind, all they are is dust in the wind.
Same old song, just a drop of water in an endless sea
All we do, crumbles to the ground, though we refuse to see

Dust in the wind, all we are is dust in the wind

[Now] Don't hang on, nothing lasts forever but the earth and sky
It slips away, and all your money won't another minute buy.

Dust in the wind, all we are is dust in the wind
Dust in the wind, everything is dust in the wind.
—"Dust in the Wind,©" Kansas, 1977

25 finally

The true appreciation of our life isn't found at a distance of a decade or more, it's understanding in the moment that the happiness you feel, the magic surrounding you like a halo or aura is worth holding onto, acknowledging all the tiny components so that much later we can recall what made the experience precious to us in the first place. Just as we're able to cope with big event after big event of stress and trauma in our lives it'll be the equivalent of the cap left off the toothpaste which pushes us over the edge to the apocalyptic meltdown seemingly about nothing.

It's the subtlety of small things we remember. Noticing keeps you alive, vital, interesting, and relevant. Beauty and reverence for transcendence drive the human soul forward in attempting to touch it, observe it, capture 'it' if only in our head, acknowledging that beauty has touched us sometimes with an outpouring of tears is what makes life complete. Capturing a special moment, however fleeting, in your head, imprinting it on your heart, gives us a liberty to return to and collect the magic contents again and again.

The iconic, more than 60 years and still in business, Cardullo's along with, sadly now out of business, the Curious George & Friends in Harvard Square was particularly special to me for the memories created one day with my dearest adopted family Pam, Bruce and my niece EJ, and her twin sisters Kate and Julia. I had run into Curious George and Friends and bought two faery rings (ribbon garlands with streamers) for Kate in shades of purple and blue and Julia in shades of pink and gold. The girls wore them as we ate our Cardullo's picnic sitting on the grass of Harvard Yard where Bruce went to law school. The girls were three or four at the time and after lunch I taught them how to turn cartwheels. You try to love them enough, create sunbeams and rainbows and sugar them up with the delight of helping to bake cookies with homemade frozen dough driven across three states at Christmas, you are purposefully eccentric enough in your behaviour to stand out so they introduce you to all their friends in 2nd grade with "this is Aunt Terri" to be met with a chorus of 60 little voices saying "HI AUNT TERRI!"; their now nearly adult friends who I see less frequently still greet me the same way and with hugs. The truth is no matter the effort put in none of us have a crystal ball when it comes to what will 'stick' with little kids. Bruce had taken the girls to interview at university campus' in Massachusetts and I walked into Kate's bedroom to deliver clean laundry only to discover the faery rings of that special day in Cambridge; I confess I never expected a high school senior (even one I love with my whole heart) to hold onto such a thing as a thirteen year old faery ring, but there it was the perfect evidence of a memory we all shared. For a moment they are four again, the curled ribbons dance on their little heads in the sunlight as they run around until they drop of exhaustion and my heart bursts with love all over again. Oh, Katie, thank you honey for holding onto the faery rings!

The morning after. Not what you are thinking, but rather the morning after the first night of my first visit to Paris. Oh. My. Head. Rule number one—eat.

If I am not still intoxicated then surely I am more wickedly hung-over than ever in my life from the post ballet, Bacchanalian indulgence on an empty stomach of Bellini's and (many) shared bottles of Veuve Cliquot© at Harry's American Bar©. This unplanned, stumbled upon, because I had quasi-memorized the street map and knew we would be reasonably safe walking to Place de la Concorde to see the Obelisk of Luxor at 11PM and we might find food on the way, and ensuing outrageously loud, pure hedonistic pleasure outing complete with a request (my first and only) by a French banker with a name of Olivier St. Croix to drink from my black patent heels and a bartender's threat to call Les Gendarmes if I did not control my party . . . for the record I had no previous knowledge of any the people for which I was suddenly being held responsible, including the four young women loudly singing their school anthems beneath the nearly ancient pennants of their respective Seven Sisters colleges or the dweeb reading Gibbons Fall of the Roman Empire two tables away who could not be cajoled into joining us. At breakfast the teeny glass of freshly squeezed orange juice placed before me wasn't going to do it, thorough recovery demands no less than a litre. It takes 10 minutes of dialogue with the owner of the patisserie that I really do WANT as much as NEED that much juice and a litre of sparkling water, but no café au lait.

I had left our days' itinerary in the competent hands of a (nearly native) friend of a friend who had been a Parisian tour guide while studying chemical engineering. Sacré-Coeur was on the list for the incredible view from the top but before I took the stairs to the top I rode the carousel. It wasn't the Louvre or Sacré-Coeur or Palais Garnier or the chocolat at Angelina's that made this January trip extraordinary for me (though all that is treasured and then some) but the point where actually riding my third Belle Époque era antique wooden carousel in a single day became a reality. Isn't the very reason we travel is to explore and (hopefully) recapture the delight we had as children discovering something for the first time? By the way, the City of Light is filled with carousels, at the Tuileries, near the Eiffel Tower, at the Jardin du Luxumbourg, Parc de la Villette and at the Gare Montparnasse to identify a few. The grey, icy-cold weather might not be everyone's ideal for jumping on a prancing wooden horse ever spinning around in circles to a calliope but I had company—just not from my small group of friends—in the form 'other' five year olds! Only one other time in my life had I managed three different carousel rides in a single day and that effort took nearly 12 hours and driving across two New England states to accomplish. In Paris we managed to walk between two, the small paper ticket nearly identical the world over, humankind bound by common experience of reaching for the golden ring and sometimes, thankfully, grabbing it.

Happiness isn't found any more or less than unhappiness, each ebb and flow through our lives. Ideally, the focus shouldn't be "I know I will be happy when . . ." but rather learning to live in the present with a mindfulness that makes our ability to express, "this is happiness, this moment, right now" a daily occurrence. Even so, repeated exposure to a single activity makes the totality a blur inseparable from attending every other opera, baseball game or carousel ride. How we do, is as important as how we remember. Does it matter how many Dave Matthews concerts you've seen if not a single thing about one of those concerts can stand distinct from the hundreds of hours attending various venues? No, it does not. What stands apart is not 2 hours of gifted musical talent or the virtuosity of his 16:43 minute encore in

Pittsburgh's PNC Ballpark but being able to celebrate the twins 16th birthday in this way. Forever cherished (for me) will be the delight on my nieces Kate and Julia faces, the walk back to our small hotel and how many Facebook postings were logged during and post-concert, along with their continued hilarity over the regional hamburger joint drive-thru attendant question about mayonnaise. Don't ask.

How are you going to live from this moment forward? Are you going to continue to rush around filling up your hours and days and years with activity that becomes blurred as your frenetic effort to numb your life with over indulgence and mindless consumption? Or can you possibly embrace the 'less is more' when coupled with powerfully intentional approach?

I hope your path becomes as richly embellished and lush as my own. I send you blessings to realise a life that is abundant in ways you think belong only to other people. I bid you to be grateful for every breath, every raindrop, each hug and kiss. To truly know that 'enough' is all you really need.

To live content with small means;
To seek elegance rather than luxury,
And refinement rather than fashion;
To be worthy, not respectable; and
Wealthy, not rich; to study hard, think quietly, talk gently, act frankly . . . to listen to
stars and buds, to babes and sages, with open heart; await occasions,
hurry never . . . this is my symphony.
—William Henry Channing, 1810-1884, This Is To Be My Symphony

acknowledgements & credits

Copyrights, trademarks and registered marks belong to the respective individuals and corporations legally holding registration to the products, songs, books, and corporations identified herein in the United States as well as internationally.

The music which plays as the sound track of my life, created by talents from the 11th century (Hildegard von Bingen), 15th century (John Dowland) and Baroque era giants Mozart, Liszt, Beethoven, Brahams to Mahalia Jackson, Glenn Miller, Benny Goodman and their orchestras, Elvis, Bobby Darin, Johnny Mercer and Johnny Cash and the contemporary efforts of Paul Odette, Sting, Chris Isaak, Florence and The Machine and many, many more a debt of gratitude for all the enormous pleasure your artistic expressions have provided.

The influence of quite literally thousands of books, read over a span forty-five years, has fashioned who I have become as an individual as well as the very nature of this book. As such I have purposefully noted the influence of such authors, living and long since deceased, and their respective works as might help define the mysteries of the human condition in reading them directly throughout **All That I Need**. In addition to the following short list may I suggest Watty Piper's quintessential children's tale of The Little Engine That Could first published in 1930 (which I am grateful to have been given as a child and then later as an adult, a first edition), Harold Lamb's sweeping Omar Khayyam and Alexandre Dumas' epic novel of reinvention The Count of Monte Cristo first published between

 225

1844 and 1845: each serve to remind us what is possible when we reach inside ourselves to overcome what obstacles lay immediately before us.

Amongst them, but certainly not limited to:
Under The Tuscan Sun, (at home in Italy), Frances Mayes, 1996, Broadway Books

Mrs Delany & Her Circle edited by Mark Laird and Alicia Weisberg-Roberts, 2009, Yale Center for British Art, Sir John Soane's Museum in association with Yale University Press, and *The Paper Garden, An Artist* (Begins Her Life's Work) at 72, Molly Peacock, 2010, Bloomsbury

Michel de Montaigne—The Complete Essays ,1993, Penguin Classics

Epicurus to Epicticus: Studies in Hellenistic and Roman Philosophy, A.A. Long 2006, Oxford University Press, USA

Shahnameh (The Epic of Kings), Abolqasem Ferdowsi, translation by Dick Davis, 2007, Penguin Classics

The History of the Lives of Abeillard and Heloisa (et al) from *The Collection of Amboise* by the Rev. Joseph Berington Volumes I & II published J.J. Tourneisen 1793

about the author

Ms Fritschi is an international award winning marketing communications professional. Her communications career began as an amateur boxing tournament coordinator. She served as the finance director for two Congressional campaigns and spent 16 years working in the high technology space including Fortune 50 firms prior to launching Thistle & Broom, a geo-politically exclusive, Fair Trade based e-commerce site. **All That I Need, or Live Like a Dog With Its Head Stuck Out the Car Window** is her first book. Ms Fritschi splits her time between Rochester, New York, and Edinburgh Scotland.

a note on the type

If it's good enough for Dante, Dr. Seuss and J.K. Rowling . . .

All That I Need text is set in the Garamond typeface. This old-style serif typeface—created by Claude Garamond (c.1480-1561) and first used for Francis I King of France—is widely regarded as to be amongst the most legible of all major typefaces. It has also been noted that Garamond uses less ink in printing so it seems it's environmentally friendly! But personally I find it fascinating that Garamond typeface has been used for Dr. Seuss, J.K. Rowling's *Harry Potter* books in the United States and The Everyman's Library edition of Dante's *The Divine Comedy*. The only complete set of the original Garamond dyes and matrices can be found in Antwerp, Belgium, at the Plantin-Moretus Museum.

 229

23418933R00134

Made in the USA
Charleston, SC
22 October 2013